Myrsini Lambraki

CRETAN CUISINE
for everyone

CONTENTS

TITLE / CRETAN CUISINE FOR EVERYONE - **AUTHOR** / Myrsini Lambraki - **COPYRIGHT** / Myrsini Edition
22, ILARIONOS KATSOULI str. Mastabas 713 05 Heraklion, Crete - Tel.& Fax: 0030 2810 210052
CELL PHONE: 6945. 468190 E-MAIL: mirsini@herforthnet.gr - **COPYRIGHT** © 2005
FIRST PUBLISHED IN GREECE / March 2005 - **ISBN**: 960-92291-3-1 - **PHOTOGRAPHS** / Douwe Hoogstins, Myrsini Lambraki - **FOOD STYLING** / Spiros Mprilakis
TRANSLATION / George Trialonis - **LAYOUT** / MKS Advertising Tel: 0030 2810 341986– **PRINTING** / TYPOKRETA Tel: 0030 2810 380882

Introduction to Crete

Lying in the southernmost area of Greece, Crete charms its visitors with the beauty of its hinterland, the impulsive nature of its people, its variegated and colourful landscapes, the plethora of its products, but most importantly, with its delectable cuisine that forms the nucleus of the world acclaimed Mediterranean Diet. The Cretan culinary habits have deep roots in history. For example, the diet of the Cretans is based on olive oil, fresh greens and vegetables, fruits, cereals and legumes. This is particularly true of people living in the hinterland. But you can find this out for yourselves by choosing any dish from the scores of dishes served or offered as a treat throughout the island.

Crete: Wise and Delectable Nutrition

Olive oil, fish, greens, vegetables, fruits, nuts, cheese, even meat and wine in moderate quantities are currently considered the constituents of a healthy diet for all people. The secret for a healthy life cannot be found in a diet low in fats, but in a diet that offers the optimal balance in fatty acids. This kind of diet is the cultural product of Cretans!

The Cretan cuisine uses natural products: olive oil, dried fruits, wild greens and herbs which, in moderate quantities offer just the right amount of fatty acids and other nutrients that inhibit the development of cancer cells.

There are greens, for example the purslane, which are consumed in relatively large amounts, particularly during the summer months. Owing to purslane's linoleic acid, the heart is fortified against various diseases. Other herbs or vegetables, e.g. the *Taraxacum Officinalis*, are excellent blood purifiers offering also other benefits relating to blood (they balance blood sugar levels, etc.). Scientists believe that the nettle, a herb that has been "decommissioned" from the Cretan cuisine, offers vitamins (B complex) which prevent the development of cancer tumors. The oil in the dried fruits contains fatty acids, e.g. a-linoleic, which promotes cellular development and function. However, the good health of Cretans, and the peoples in the broader Mediterranean area, has been attributed mainly to the large consumption of raw olive oil. This precious substance is mentioned over and over again in ancient Greek scripts, e.g. in the Linear B' tablets of Knosos and Phaestos. In one of these tablets, the olive oil is found listed among other Cretan products: figs, honey, wine and sage.

This liberal use of raw olive oil, combined with the long-term consumption of food high in complex carbohydrates (nuts and legumes) and vegetable fibre (fruits and vegetables) have placed the Cretans and the Japanese at the top of the longevity list, proving also that healthy food can also be delectable.

THE GASTRONOMIC CHART OF CRETE

Visitors to Crete will be amazed by the vista of scores of taverns dotting favourite beaches, tucked under perennial eucalyptus trees, lacing village squares or in the center of towns. These taverns, as well as cafés and ouzo joints, offer delicious food and delicacies.

If you visit the prefecture of *Hania* in a summer month,

'Sfakianés pites' (thin, local pies) and *'Toùrta'* (a kind of pie stuffed with three kinds of soft cheese and meat. Another delicious dish is the *'gamopilafo'* (wedding pilaf) served with four kinds of meat.

do not miss the chance to taste the *'kolokythoboureko'*, topped with sesame; the *'kalitsounia'*, scented with mint leaves; the pudding (*'staka'*), made from fresh milk; the octopus with fennel and the salad from wild 'stamnagathi'.

Driving south in the same prefecture, towards Sfakia, *Ayia Roumeli* and *Fragocastelo*, you could ask for

East of *Hania* lies the prefecture of Rethymnon. The capital by the same name has a charm of its own, particularly during the summer when cultural activities take place (the Renaissance festival, etc.). The old port evokes warm feelings and a sense of trust and homeliness. Do not resist the temptation to indulge in the local food; ask for the kinds of soft cheese available – feta cheese and yogurt. The lamb served in restaurants and taverns is delicious. It is cooked with *'avronies'* or plant roots (*'volvous'*). Also, omelet with asparagus tastes heavenly. Well, when it comes to

Cretan food, taste loses much of its subjective character and warrants such comments. If you like seafood, you could order octopus, squid or cuttlefish on charcoal. For desert, the watermelon from the area of *Panormo* is juicy and refreshing.

The prefecture of Heraklion is east of Rethymnon. The capital by the same name offers an international atmosphere and is a favourite destination for millions of guests from all over the world. Consequently, in addition to the local cuisine you can also find more familiar dishes. However, why take the familiar track when on vacation? Try something different. In the center of the town, by the Lions' Square, you can find delicious pies (sweet or sour) at *Kirkor* or *Salkitzis*. The original owners were of Armenian origin, while their descendants are the proud keepers of a tradition in cream and cheese pie making that is eight centuries old.

Tradition plays a major role in food preparation as it combines knowledge of nature and a sense of measure. This combination has given rise to a range of traditional dishes that are both tasty and nourishing, e.g. urchin salad, stuffed vine leaves (*'dolmadakia'*), stuffed vegetables (tomatoes, eggplants, the flowers of marrows, potatoes), fried snails, animal entrails in lemon sauce (*'gardoumia'*), cuttlefish cooked in its ink. *'Skordoulakoi'* (plant roots) and green salads offer unique palatable experiences. The same is true concerning other dishes which may be particular to a specific location of the island. For example, in the Psiloritis range area you can order spaghetti topped with cream cheese (*'anthotyros'*). In this area the spaghetti precedes roast meat from free range goats. The desert to follow comprises sour pies topped with

thyme honey.

To wrap up our gastronomic *tour de force*, let us 'visit' the prefecture of Lassithi, the easternmost prefecture of Crete. Picking an earlier hint, this prefecture too has its own culinary practices – the result of tradition, quality of produce and ingenuity of the inhabitants.

This prefecture is renowned for its preserves made from fresh fruit; the sweets from dried fruits (almond nuggets and pies, etc.), the *'soumada'* and other deserts that combine local products and feminine imagination (e.g. cheese pies and *'patouda'*).

The combinations of fresh fish with vegetables (e.g. okras with fish) are stunning, particularly in the town of Siteia. We recommend *Skarus* (parrotfish) stew with vegetables in tomato sauce.

The inhabitants of this prefecture believe that prime quality fish and other seafood resourced from the Cretan Sea were enjoyed by the dignitaries of the *Zakros* palace on Crete and the Pharaohs of Egypt. To conclude your palatable tour to the Cretan cuisine, you could order a carafe of refreshing raki and *xerotigano* and/or *anevato* scented with lemon leaves from Siteia.

Finger-liking Cretan preparations

The traditional cuisine of Crete is the result of very long experience that has managed to preserve the sensorial qualities and terminology of Cretan dishes throughout the centuries. The culinary art of the island is based on simple techniques and original combinations of the ingredients involved in the preparation of a wide range

of dishes.

The ultimate aim has always been the enhancement of tastes and nutritious benefits from all products used in the making of the various dishes. The products that form the spine of the Cretan cuisine are: olive oil, cereals, wine, vegetables, dairy products and wild greens/herbs.

Summer preparations require discrete combinations of ingredients, such that make an optimal use of garden produce, delicious dairy products, fish, mollusks, urchins, crispy cooked goat meat and fresh fruits. A case in point is the delicious Hania tart made from three different kinds of cheese, mint and lamb – all wrapped in fluffy phyllo dough topped with sesame.

There are 72 kinds of edible herbs/greens that are consumed raw, boiled or braised. These herbs/greens are found in abundance in autumn and winter, when there is a riot of vegetation owing to rains. In summer the inhabitants enjoy the purslane, open-air vegetables (tomatoes, cucumbers, blites, nightshade, marrows) and vine leaves.

As regards fish, the salt cod, octopus and cuttlefish are very favourite with the Cretans. In addition, the island offers classical kakavia (shore dinner) dishes, but my favourite is the one made in the Siteia area, which includes braised potatoes.

In addition to mouth-watering preserves made from fresh fruits and nuts, the locals and visitors alike have a sweet tooth also for the little pies known as *kalitsounia*

and *xerotigana*. The former are made from sweet or sour cheese, '*myzéthra*', spices in phyllo dough. The latter are made from thin phyllo dough twisted in complex formations. Both are topped with honey or grape juice syrup. The *xerotigana* are offered to guests in wedding and christening ceremonies.

The hearts of Cretans are among the strongest in the world...

The Cretan diet is based on olive oil. This precious juice

has a high content in monounsaturated fatty acids. Cretans, in contrast to northern Europeans, use a lot of olive oil in the preparation of their meals. This explains the fact that cardiovascular diseases are rare among the population of Crete in comparison to other countries where animal fats (butter, margarine, lard, etc.), i.e. saturated fatty acids, are used.

Testimonies and proof of the above are provided both by acclaimed travelers, who visited Crete in the past centuries, and by scientists who conducted comparative research in nutrition. They all note the love of Cretans for olive oil. Actually, the travelers reported that Cretan meals "float" in the precious juice of the olive tree. What is more, the Cretan diet has been under the international limelight distinguishing it from its Mediterranean counterpart in terms of olive oil content:

"The Cretan diet is based mainly in foodstuff of vegetative origin: cereals, vegetables, fruit and olive oil ... Olives and olive oil contribute significantly to the vitality of the Cretans. Visitors to Crete are impressed by the fact that Cretan food virtually 'floats' in olive oil. This juice finds extravagant applications in the local kitchen. It is the sine qua non for salads, soups and vegetable dishes... The consumption of olive in such large amounts is characteristic of Cretans who consume a lot more olive oil than people living in other regions of Greece." (extracted from a research report by the Rockefeller Institute, USA.).

The Mediterranean diet, a very broad term encompassing the nutritional habits of the peoples in the Mediterranean basin, received international acclaim following the publication of the Seven Countries Study. This study established that Cretans were found to manifest the lowest mortality rates from coronary heart diseases in relation to other population groups that participated in the study. This find was attributed to a diet rich in olive oil (100gr per capita on average per day) which constitutes one third of the energy intake required by the human body.

Recent scientific evidence shows that high consumption of olive oil not only reduces the levels of LDL cholesterol in blood, but also inhibits the oxidation of LDL owing to the effects of antioxidant substances, e.g. tocophenols, polyphenols, etc. in olive oil. In addition, the olive oil does not reduce HDL levels, in contrast to the polyunsaturates (vegetable oils). The latter are rich in hyperoxides whose oxidating effects in lipoproteins is the prime cause for the deposit of lipids in the walls of the arteries.

Cretan (Mediterranean) Diet – Research – Recommendations

Research interest in any gastronomic heritage is rather limited. Nevertheless, the few papers published are interesting in terms of their folkloric content. What is missing is field research in specific nutritional customs and habits that are worth preserving or imitating. A case in point is the gastronomic heritage of Crete whose effects on human health and happiness render it a paragon of a diet. The traditional diet of Cretans, which is a way of life, meets the scientific criteria for an optimal/ideal diet, a nutritional standard that promotes health and prevents the onset of diseases. This was the conclusion of the Seven Countries Study conducted by Dr. Ancel Keys and collaborators in 1960. They studied a number of population groups (cohorts) in Europe, USA, Japan and Greece. The cohorts from Greece were pooled from the islands of Crete and Corfu. Crete was chosen as it met the study's requirement for a location where people remained faithful to a traditional way of life and nutrition. Corfu was selected on account of the fact that it was the first region in Greece to adopt western dietary habits. Data were collected on the causes of death for each group during 15 years of follow-up, and the relationship between antioxidant nutrient intake and mortality rates from heart diseases and cancer growths were assessed. The study showed that Cretans had the lowest mortality rates from heart diseases and cancer. During the period of 15-year follow-up the deaths from cardiovascular (CVD) diseases were: 38 for Crete, 132 for Japan, 202 for Corfu, 462 for Italy , 773 for the USA, and 972 for Finland.

On the basis of these results the English epidemiologist Blackburn spoke of the Cretan miracle. The lowest mortality rates for the Cretan group were attributed to their way of life and nutrition. Thirty one years following the onset of this study the University of Crete (department of Social Medicine) established that in 1991 half (50%) of the Cretan participants in the study

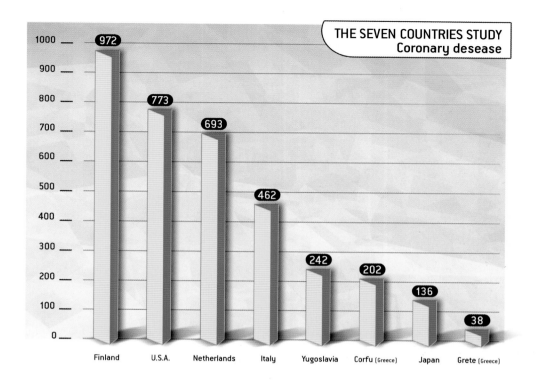

1000 — 972
900 —
800 — 773
700 — 693
600 —
500 — 462
400 —
300 —
242
200 — 202
136
100 —
38
0 —

Finland   U.S.A.   Netherlands   Italy   Yugoslavia   Corfu (Greece)   Japan   Grete (Greece)

were still alive, while all participants from Finland had passed away.

One might ask: what was the particular way of life of Cretans in the late '50s and early '60s, when the study was in full swing? Well, most of Cretans were involved with manual work, mainly in the fields. They also walked approximately 13 km on average daily. This increased physical activity was combined with a diet high in calorific value. Olive oil provided 1/3 of daily energy requirements per person. The typical Cretan diet consisted mainly of cereals (bread), legumes, vegetables, fruits and olive oil. Little cheese and very little meat or fish, plus one or two glasses of wine in each meal were also on the daily agenda of Cretans. Now, another question might be: were the Cretans much wiser than other Europeans or Americans to have adopted this kind of healthy diet? Certainly not. The physical activities – farming/fishing, walking long distances, etc. – were the standard way of living on the island. What about their diet? The answer is that

Cretans had no alternative diets. They had to consume what they themselves produced – and they did an excellent job with their home-grown and field products. In fact, the palatable Cretan dishes were the result of female imagination. The physical activities involving the growing and collection of foodstuff was mainly the task of males, while cooking was the task of females. This division of tasks and roles was part of the Cretan family organization – a tradition. The nature of the local cuisine provided nourishment and strength to Cretan families, the majority of which were poor people, devastated by wars and conflict. As the industrial wave nudged in their way of life, family bonds were loosened (increased mobility of women and children, etc), which brought significant changes in the Cretans' dietary habits. During the last few decades the old way of life on Crete has changed significantly. The traditional modes of meal preparation were infiltrated by western modalities which undermined the health of the local population: CVR incidents and cancer growths increased

to epidemic proportions. One more question: are we entitled to demand of people to return to a traditional way of life and nutrition? An affirmative answer would be unwise, if not absurd, in spite of the fact that the benefits of the traditional Cretan diet have been corroborated by scientific research. However, we are confident that knowledge of this diet will spur individual adjustments by interested individuals. Such knowledge and adjustments are warranted given the publicity the Cretan diet has

received and of the fact that certain western nutritional standards are implicated in health and economic problems. Given the fact that economic hardship has spread to global proportions, it would be wiser to substitute a portion of our meat allowance with fish. Let me remind you that Japan ranked second to Crete in terms of lower mortality rates from cardiovascular diseases. This is attributed to the fact that the Japanese are avid consumers of fish. We are not sure why fish is

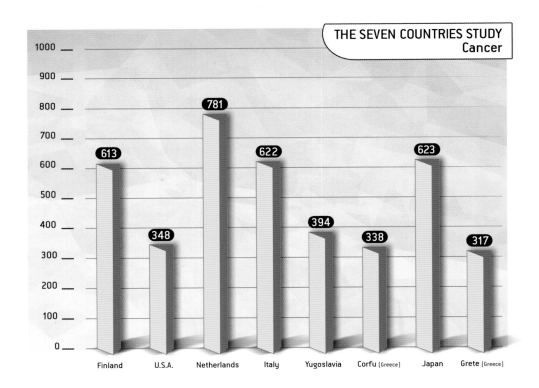

THE SEVEN COUNTRIES STUDY
Cancer

Finland 613 — U.S.A. 348 — Netherlands 781 — Italy 622 — Yugoslavia 394 — Corfu (Greece) 338 — Japan 623 — Grete (Greece) 317

good for health; perhaps it is the fish oil.

The fact with olive oil is that it inhibits the oxidation of "good" cholesterol, HDL. Consequently, the byproducts of oxidation do not clog the arteries. At the same time the levels of HDL cholesterol remain high. We can achieve the same effect if we substituted meat with fish in our diet.

Standards of living that are closer to the Cretan way of life also involve increased physical activity and the consumption of fresh and unadulterated products of land and sea.

In 1988 Serge Renault, director of the nutrition and cardiology department at the National Institute for Health Research in Lyon, France, conducted a research with 600 subjects that had suffered a cardiac infarct. Half of his subjects were instructed to follow the Cretan diet, i.e. olive oil, vegetables, fruit, little meat and fish, little butter. The diet of the other half followed the recommendations of the American Cardiology Society. The study was originally scheduled to conclude in five years, but was interrupted in a period of 27 months as a result of significant developments: sixteen subjects from the latter group had died, as against three from the former group. At a later time, after the study had been stopped, eight subjects under the American Cardiology regime, suffered a sudden cardiac arrest. This study corroborated the Keys' et al. postulates and findings that nutrition can be a major factor of health and life expectancy. Another finding that changed the perception of experts about the source of calories was that in spite of recommendations for 30% calories intake from fatty substances, the Cretan diet, which proved healthier than other diets, offers 40% of calories from olive oil. Comprising monounsaturates, vitamins and other antioxidant elements, the olive oil shields the heart from diseases and the human body from cancer growths. The effects of very expensive medication is half that obtained by observing the precepts of the Cretan diet.

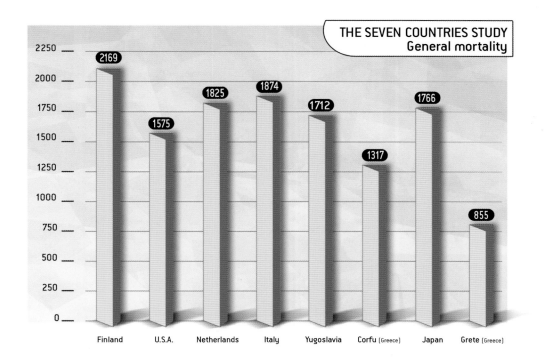

THE SEVEN COUNTRIES STUDY
General mortality

The gastronomic terms used in Crete

CHEESE

GRUYERE: The Cretan gruyere, *graviera*, is a large, hard type cheese, the finest in Greece. A wheel of gruyere may weigh from 6 to 25 kilos and has a natural rind. It has a firm consistency and a pale yellow colour. When you take a slice out of it you will notice small holes (eyes) the size of lentils, or even larger. This cheese is made from unpasteurized milk. The product metrics are the following: humidity 38%, fats 38.4%, salt 1.5%. The Cretan gruyere matures in three months. Cretan gruyere of the finest quality is produced from sheep's milk on the mountainous areas during the months of spring. However, goat's milk may also be used, which gives gruyere of lower quality.

KEFALOTYRI: This is one of the finest and most famous spicy cheeses of Crete. It is firm and dry offering a slightly sharp finish to an already distinct sheep's milk, particularly when the cheese is over one year old and has been produced in offhand storerooms on the mountains.

SOUR *MYZYTHRA*: soft cheese with sharp, sour taste and paste or granular texture. This type of cheese could be classified among the table cheeses, but is mainly used in the production of pies ('*sarikópita*') and pastries ('*kalitsoùnia*'), etc.

MYZYTHRA or _ANTHOTYRO_: In eastern Crete the *myzithra* is snowy white, soft, sweet and rather fatty. This is made from the whey of ewe's or goat's milk, or a combination of the two. It is consumed

as table cheese or served with honey and dry fruits. Also, it is the basic ingredient for 'kalitsoùnia'. When sprinkled with salt and left to mature in dry air, it gets harder, with a spicy taste and concentrated texture. This new cheese is called 'anthótyros'. In western Crete the term 'anthótyros' is reserved for soft and fresh cheese, and for the hard version of *myzithra*. In central and eastern Crete anthóyros is considered one of the grand table cheeses. When dry, it is normally grated over spaghetti boiled in meat stock.

TYROZOULI: A small size, home–made cheese made from goat's milk. The milk is boiled to coagulate in 30-32oC with the addition of vinegar, lemon juice or the milky latex of figs. *The tyrozouli* is strained in baskets and dried in the air. It has a semi–hard texture and very pleasant taste.

MALAKA: A compact soft cheese very much like the Italian *mozzarella*. It is mildly sweet in taste and elastic in texture. It is made only in spring and consumed as is or as an ingredient to *kalitsounia* and meat pies.

PICTOGALO of Hania: soft cheese with creamy texture and mildly sour and cool taste. It is produced only in the prefecture of Hania and constitutes the basic ingredient for meat pies and *bouréki*. It is also a table cheese, which is spread over hard bread (rusks). This cheese came under the label "Protected Designation of Origin" in 1996.

STAKA: This is a kind of roux made from the cream

of milk (or the residue of clarified butter) with an addition of flour. Warm the milk or butter; add one or two tablespoons of flour and whisk, adding a little water to dissolve the remaining floury solids. You will get a pale creamy substance and a thicker one around the former (the butter). The cream is spread over bread slices while the butter is used for thickening all sorts of dishes including soups and sauces, even fried eggs.

PIES

SARIKOPITES: Pies in spiral shape stuffed with sour myzithra. These pies are fried in a lot of olive oil and served with honey. These pies were named after the Cretan kerchief (headband) known as "sariki".

KALITSOUNIA: These little pies are made from soft (usually sweet and at times sub-sour) myzithra in the areas of Siteia, Herakion, and Rethymnon. Their shape is reminiscent of little oil lamps, hence their alternative name, 'lycharakia'. Also, they may be of triangular shape. In Hania the kalitsounia are salty and made from herbs or fresh onions (*hortokalitsouna* or *kremidokalitsouna*) or with a mixture of cheeses and a lot of mint.

BOUREKI: this is a kind of salty pie made exclusively in the prefecture of Hania. It is made from grated vegetable marrows, potatoes, sour myzithra or whey cheese and mint.

mixture of strong vinegar, cumin and pepper for a few days. The meat chunks are "cured" in the vinegar and smoked over assorted herbs to ultimately acquire a piquant taste closer to the aromas of sage and cypress tree. In Rethymnon and Hania the sausages are made from freshly cut pork meat, but they are not smoked.

TSILADIA: Another name for this delicacy is

MEAT

ANTIKRISTO: This way of cooking meat combines a "primitive" process with a delicious result: large cuts of meat, usually lamb or goat, are pierced through bare tree-branches fixed on the ground around a bon fire. The meat is cooked slowly in the heat for 4–5 hours. This way of cooking meat is customary in the area of *Mylopotamos* and in the mountainous regions of *Mt. Psiloreitis.*

OFTO: meat from lamb or goat. It is first sprinkled with a hefty amount of salt, then roasted in wood-fired ovens or on open-air fire.

MENOUZES: This is more like the *'kokoretsi'* (skewered assorted meat cuts) of mainland Greece. On Crete the meat pieces are the same (animal entrails, intestines, etc.), albeit cut to larger sizes, while the skewers used are much smaller – 20 to 30 cm long.

APAKI: This is smoked griskin – a tender slice of meat eaten raw or mixed with herbs in an omelet.

SAUSAGES: The traditional sausages in Crete are made from finely sliced pork meat immersed in a

"pechtë", meaning thick; otherwise known as pork jelly. It consists of assorted pork meat (taken from the animal's head and feet). When the meat simmers, a thick juice is produced that coagulates to jelly. The meat is cooked in a variety of spices: cumin, bay leaves and bigarade juice. It is an excellent Christmas delicacy.

SFAKIANO YACHNI (STEW): slices of lamb or goat meat braised in a lot of olive oil and a little wine.

CAPRICO: pork shoulder blade placed on dry vine branches and cooked slowly in the oven. When done, the meat is wrapped in oil-proof sheets with lemon leaves for 4–5 hous, then served cold.

SWEETS/DESERTS – BREAD

PATOUDA: A desert made in eastern Crete: small, bite-size rusks stuffed with a mixture of currants, almonds and grated orange rind.

XEROTIGANA: fritters made from very thin dough coiled by hand and cooked in olive oil. They are topped with honey and sprinkled with chopped nuts.

KOUKOUVAYA (OWL): another name for the famous Cretan dakos. A round barley rusk that is virtually dripping in olive oil, topped with grated tomato and crumbled feta cheese or sour *myzithra* (*xynomizithra*).

EPTAZYMA: another type of rusk the basic ingredient of which is sour-dough made from pulverized

chopped and mixed with other ingredients.

XOBLIASTES GAMOCOULOURES:

this is a round, decorated bread (the phrase actually means broidered wedding bread) made by skillful women. The decorations represent small flowers, serpents, leaves, trees and human figures − all made from dough.

chick-peas. You can find these rusks in *Heraklion*, *Ayios Nikolaos* and *Siteia*.

ANOPOLITICO RUSK: an excellent, mildly sweet rusk made only in the village of *Anopolis* in *Sfakia* and in *Askyfou*. Its distinguishing taste is the result of coriander, a generous quantity of which is finely

"IONIA": THE OLDEST RESTAURANT OF HERAKLION

This restaurant is a true representative of an urban cuisine that is in the brink of extinction today. Following the Hellenic Disaster of Asia Minor in 1921, late *Ioannis Georgantelis* sought refuge in Heraklion, Crete, in 1922. He and *Constantine Aronis* and *Andronicos Souvatsiannis* purchased the *AVEROF* restaurant and changed its name to *IONIA*. The *Georgantelis* family set their hearts to the business, employing all the culinary skills acquired in their homeland, Asia Minor. Soon the *IONIA* restaurant became synonymous with good and healthy eating.

In 1992 the *IONIA* was acquired by a young man, *Mr. Manolis Kokolakis*, whose intention is to revive the traditional, urban cuisine. A powerful ally is his son and chef *Sossos*, who emulates the skills of a former *IONIA* chef, *Michael Renios*. In addition to the classic, red sauce dishes, the menu of *IONIA* includes delectable broad beans, chick-pea puree, lima beans in red sauce, artichokes a la polita, and many more.

The "display window" of *IONIA* is a colourful 'palette' and an invitation to dinner for all fans of homemade food.

SHEEP SHEARING: THE CRETAN SHEPHERDS' FESTIVAL

As the season of spring yields to the hot months of summer, the shepherds of Crete lead their flocks to higher, mountainous locations for sheering. Shepherds usually invite friends to attend the sheering and have fun in the ensuing feast. If you are lucky enough, you may also be invited in a sheep sheering festival. The experience is unique. It goes without saying that the shepherd's extended family is not only in attendance but also has important tasks as host. They set the feast table; serve the boiled meat (*zigouri*), the pilaf or spaghetti and *ofto* meat. The feast begins as soon as the sheering is done. A local orchestra is present to entertain the guests who enjoy the home-made wine, the *raki* and the meat in the sounds of such local instruments as the lyre and the lute.

The olive tree and its oil in prehistoric times

The cultivation of olive trees has been an ancient practice in the Mediterranean basin. The products of this cultivation, olives and olive oil, have been used to meet basic dietary needs. It has been common knowledge among the peoples of the Mediterranean that the leaves of the olive tree and olive oil have therapeutic qualities. Olive oil was used as offering to domestic gods.

The Greeks have been using the olive tree products for thousands of years. Until a few years ago the olive oil was almost exclusively used in all meal preparations by the inhabitants of Crete, Peloponnese and the Aegean islands. It comes as no surprise then that the olive tree was revered by the people who benefited from it. The olive tree was considered holy and as such it entered the Greek folk tradition.

OLIVE OIL IN MINOAN COOKING POTS

The Minoans and the people of the Mycenaean period, during the second and the third millennium before Christ, used olive oil for practical as well as religious purposes. As far as the cooking uses are concerned, we now have quite a good idea, even though there is no written evidence. A chemical analysis of Minoan cooking pots showed that the people of that time used olive oil in their cooking!

Tablets found at Knossos record deliveries of oil along with other basic food products, such as barley, figs, wine, honey and flour, which were sent out to unknown receivers, maybe even members of some kind of priesthood.

WHY IS OLIVE OIL THE BEST FATTY SUBSTANCE

(Olive Oil Campaign by the European Union)

The natural juice from olives is clearly the best in comparison to any other fatty substance, animal (lard, butter) or vegetable (corn oil, Soya-bean oil, palm oil, sunflower oil) utilized in human nutrition.
Olive oil offers unique nutritional, aromatic and biological features that render it an excellent and irreplaceable supplement in relation to other animal and vegetable oils.
• Olive oil, particularly the extra virgin, is a natural juice extracted from the olive fruits under natural processes (crushing, pressure, centrifugation, collection) without any additives or preservatives and no further processing. It can be consumed immediately after collection, as is the case with all fresh fruit juices.
• The olive oil offers significant aromatic substances and other elements that make it tastier than all other fatty substances.
• Olive oil is of average calorific value in comparison to other fatty substances.
• Owing to its increased content in polyphenols and tocopherols, olive oil is resistant to rancidity and oxidation.
• Since it is rich in monounsaturated acids and natural antioxidants, olive oil is better for frying than any other seed oil.
• The chemical make up of olive oil is ideal for the human body. It offers natural antioxidant substances that are highly significant for health.

OLIVE OIL THE SECRET OF HEALTH

It has been established that olive oil shields the human body against cardiovascular diseases, cancer growths, diabetes and other diseases. More and more research is being conducted in nutrition with results corroborating the significance of olive oil in maintaining health and preventing diseases.

BAD CHOLESTEROL:

The consumption of olive oil instead of other fats reduces the concentration of LDL cholesterol in blood without decreasing the levels of HDL, the so-called "bad" and "good" cholesterol respectively.

TRIGLYCERIDES:

It has been shown that olive oil reduces the level of triglycerides in blood. A collection of bad cholesterol and triglycerides in blood can block the arteries which transport oxygen to the brain and heart. In general, olive oil protects against heart diseases.

HYPERTENSION:

Olive oil reduces blood pressure, both systolic and diastolic. Therefore it decreases the risk of heart attacks and strokes.

CANCER:

Recent studies have shown that olive oil consumption can slow down breast cancer and other types of cancer. A balanced diet with olive oil and vegetables can reduce the chances the appearance of cancer by 75%.

GASTROINTESTINAL SYSTEM:

Recent research shows that olive oil in conjunction with a healthy diet (vegetables, little meat, pulses)
Protects against cancer of the stomach
Makes the liver work better
Helps the liver to detoxify and cleanse from poisonous substances

OSTEOPOROSIS:

Olive oil assists in the maintenance of bone thickness and protects against osteoporosis.

DIABETES:

Olive oil should also be included in the treatment of diabetes.

The composition of olive oil resembles that of maternal milk and is most efficient in the development of the central nervous system in babies and children.
Olive oil contributes to the development of the bones,

especially in children and adolescents.
Olive oil, due to the antioxidant elements it contains, protects the brain and keeps it alert in old age.
Olive oil enhances skin, protecting it from sun burns.

And last but not least, I would like to offer some tips on the assessment of olive oil to those of you who may not be familiar with the subject.

ASSESSING OLIVE OIL

TASTING AT HOME...
Tasting should take place in a neutral, well-lit environment. Choose two or three different kinds and take care not to read the labels and thus be influenced. Have a piece of paper and pen ready to jot down your impressions of taste, fragrance and color. Eat a little apple or plain bread between tries to keep your palate clean.

LOOKING AT THE OLIVE OIL
Empty a little olive oil in a flute type wine glass and look at the color holding the glass up to the light. The colours may vary greatly, from dark within some range,

from dark green to pale green or to an almost transparent golden shade of green.

IS COLOR AN INDICATION OF QUALITY?
No, not always. However, as a rule of thumb, the greener the olive oil, the stronger the aroma and the richer the taste. This is due to the fact that the olives were picked at exactly the right moment – not too green and not too black. But a rich green colour can also be obtained by including a few olive leaves in the pressing of the olives. The colour improves in this manner but not the taste, which turns bitter.

USING YOUR SENSE OF SMELL
The aroma of the olive oil is a factor of its overall

condition. Hold the glass in your hand and rock the oil to and fro a couple of times, then take a whiff breathing deeply. Now ask yourselves: does it smell fresh? Is the smell strong? How can you define it?

TASTING OLIVE OIL
This is the most important step. Take a mouthful of the oil but don't swallow it yet. As in wine tasting, have the liquid circulate in your mouth, over and under your tongue and finally let it slide down your throat, letting the air out through your teeth. Try to evaluate the

acidity; is the taste bitter, sweet, sharp? The tongue tastes the bitterness, the inside of the cheeks taste the sharpness and the tip of the tongue, the sweetness.

DO ALL KINDS OF RAW OLIVE OIL TASTE THE SAME?
There is a wide range in the taste of olive oil and it is precisely these natural flavors that make olive oil so unique among other edible oils. Connoisseurs generally classify olive oil as mild (delicate, light or buttery), semi-fruity (with a stronger taste of olives) and fruity (with a full-blown olive fragrance).

FLAVORS VARY FROM ONE REGION TO ANOTHER
The climate, the soil, the weather, the harvesting methods, the type of olives, the specific location of the

olive grove, all play a significant role in the final taste of the olive oil. Just as with wine, there is a great difference in taste between all the olive oils produced in Greece, and even between the Cretan kinds. It is up to you to discover them!

PLEASANT TASTES AND SMELLS
By comparison with other edibles:
Apple: olive oil tastes of either a ripe apple or else the peel of a green apple
Grass: a scent like the one of freshly mown grass
Green leaves: a taste similar to that of unripe olives and leaves
Almond: a strong taste like the one of a fresh almond
Hay: a typical smell of some kinds of olive oil that tend to smell like hay
Fruit: fresh olive oil in particular often has a multiple aroma that brings to mind different types of fresh fruit
Lemon: a delicate unusual fragrance with a peppery taste
Sorrel: similar to the lemon fragrance, but not as definite
Spice: some kinds of olive oil leave a pungent, spicy, sweet-'n-sour taste

UNPLEASANT TASTES AND SMELLS
Rust
Earth
Metal
Mildew
Brine

COOKING WITH OLIVE OIL
In order to close my speech I would like to take a little about cooking with olive oil.

Olive oil is ideal for cooking purposes. It adds a wonderful taste to the food and makes it healthier and easier to digest. You can enjoy olive oil in a great variety of recipes, either cooked or raw; excellent for marinading meat or fish, it is ideal too for frying.

WHAT TYPE TO USE
Light and delicate dishes like poached or sautéed fish, chicken or veal, or perhaps mild flavored soups, may be better served with a milder, less fruity olive oil. Full-flavored robust dishes such as hearty stews, soups, or tomato-based sauces welcome a more fruity, flavorful olive oil, as do steamed vegetables and salads. Roasted, barbequed and braised dishes are which require high or prolonged rare cooking, it is probably

best used with fine/semi-fine olive oil because it is less rich in the volatile compounds that evaporate with heat, and may "perfume" your kitchen.

DELICIOUS WAYS TO ENJOY EXTRA VIRGIN OLIVE OIL
• Replace butter or margarine by a little plateful of olive oil in which to dip your bread or rusk.
• Add a tablespoon of olive oil to the water in which you boil your pasta: in this way, it won't stick.
• Rub a little olive oil on your hands to spread your dough to prevent sticking
• Pour a little olive oil over your potatoes before baking them to make them more crisp.
• Sprinkle olive oil on all greens, on boiled potatoes, on carrots, beans or any other vegetable and serve them with fresh parsley and spring onions.

The olive museum of Crete

The village of Kapsaliana is on the way to the town of Rethymnon, in the direction to the historic monastery of Arkadi. It is 5 km from the village of Eleftherna and 8 km from the coast. The village houses were built around an old oil mill, property of the Arkadi monastery. The entire settlement is of "high cultural value", once a glebe property of the Monastery of Arkadi with olives and olive oil production being a significant source of income.

The wooden casings on the upper floor of the oil mill bear numerous inscriptions by the hands of monks. These inscriptions make reference to olive crops in the end of the 19th century and beginning of the 20th century. The oil mill of the Arkadi monastery had been active for over 300 years.

This building complex of the oil mill is currently under radical renovation for conversion to an Olive Museum with an emphasis Crete. The Olive Museum features numerous interesting spaces, some of which are of particular interest, e.g. the main production area, the storage hall with the jars, the old mill equipment, the Cretan-type fireplace, the cell of the monk-caretaker. However, the conversion works aim to maintain the character of those spaces to thus enhance their historic and cultural significance.

Visitors will have the opportunity to educate themselves in the production of olives and olive oil as was practiced on the island from antiquity up until the mid 20th century, when this oil mill was decommissioned. In addition, the exhibits and information available will help establish in visitors the relationship between the olive tree, olive products and man. Furthermore, the Museum will be a venue for numerous events aiming to educate the public in olive trees and in the use and applications of olive oil. The following satellite facilities are also contemplated: a restaurant offering traditional food, café, bookstore, pottery shop, and greengrocer's shop stocked with local products, e.g. a variety of olives, olive paste, olive oil, herbs, etc.

OLIVES

TSAKISTES (Crushed): medium size green olives crushed whole either by stone or a metallic implement. They are kept in brine and lemon or bigarade juice for a couple of months before consumption. They have a slightly bitter taste, firm skin and a crunchy texture.

STAFIDOLIES: the term means olives resembling currants on account of the fact their skin is wrinkled, as in raisins/currants. They are large and when mature they drop from the trees for people to collect and consume. Their sweet taste is the result of a fungus that attacks the fruit. These olives cannot be preserved for a long period of time and you can find them in local markets only in the first months of the autumn.

Herbs – Vegetables – Fruits of Crete

The deceptively barren hills and mountains of Crete, the rocky landscape, thick olive groves, uncultivated plots, even the rugged coastline host a most interesting flora, a unique evolutionary crossbreed of the European, African and Asian flora. Many of the plant species endemic to Crete actually naturalized from other continents centuries ago. In particular, the Cretan flora includes 57 species native of Asia and not found anywhere else in Europe, and 231 species not encountered in mainland Greece.

In 19th century botanist M. Rikli published a list of 28 African plant species endemic to deserts and the steppe, however 8 of those were also recorded on Crete. This explains the enthusiasm of Austrian born physician–botanist F.W. Sieber who visited Crete and later wrote, "...*what impressed me most was a leafless and flowerless sprig of the capparis egyptiana. On closer examination of the stem, I concluded that I was looking at a capparis shrub. I identified the Egyptian species of capparis following examination of its golden reflexed spines. This species is not found in Europe.*"

In his three volume work "Vegetation of the Mediterranean region", M. Rikli provides a table of plant species encountered in five of the largest islands in the Mediterranean – Sicily, Sardenia, Cyprus, Corsica and Crete. He notes that although

Crete is comparatively the smallest of the five, yet it hosts the richest flora of all with more than 2,170 species. The comparison is even more compelling on the basis of the following facts: England, although double in size than Greece, hosts only 2,133 plant species, while prewar Germany and Austria numbered only 3,500 plant species.

Our information about the variety of plant species flourishing during the Minoan period on Crete is very scanty, originating mainly from archaeological excavations which yielded murals and vases with representations of fruits, trees, herbs, etc. Other

information comes from paleo–botanist research. However, we should take into account that all living organisms, including plant life, evolve through time. Therefore, known plant species today may be the evolutionary descendants of species that existed in varied forms in the remote past. Identification of past plant species is rather difficult, however, information about their applications can be deduced from their representations on excavated murals and artifacts. A vessel containing vegetable remains was found during excavations at the Minoan palace of Malia. Three kinds of fruit, corresponding to different plant species, were identified: cedar, coriander and wild fennel. Even today cedar fruits are consumed by the inhabitants of the isle of Gavdos, south of Crete. Furthermore, the rich aroma of wild fennel is much appreciated by the modern Cretan cuisine.

During the summer of 2000 new excavations at the village of Archanes by Cretan archaeologists Yiannis and Efi Sakelarakis confirmed the belief that aromatic herbs were used and traded by the Minoans. Unearthed vessels of 1 and 2 lt were probably used as containers for the kinds of herbs exported to mainland Greece and Egypt. The Minoans used the saffron crocus in their meals and in rituals. This is testified by mural representations. We now know that the saffron crocus was intensively cultivated and used up to 16th and 17th century. This is supported by the following extract from popular literature, "...Oh! Spaghetti with grated cheese and richly saffroned, ...dearest cheese pies ..." More information about the plant species of Crete comes from authors, botanists, and physicians of antiquity, e.g. Homer, Theophrastus, Dioscurides, Pliny, Galen, Diodorus and Oreivasius. On the basis of ancient literature and research the following plant species were of outmost importance for the ancients: dittany, the Cretan cypress tree, palm tree, oregano, thyme and the cedar tree.

Claudius Galen, the personal physician of Roman emperor Marcus Aurelius, reports on the unique medicinal qualities of edible Cretan herbs: "Many of the herbs cultivated in the emperor's gardens originate from Crete. Many of the greens, herbs, fruits, and seeds on this island can not be found anywhere in the world..." However, from 5th to 15th century AD we have very little information about the flora of Crete, mainly from

Cretan literature, particularly from Cretan theatrical plays. From this information we can deduce that Cretans consumed considerable quantities of wild greens and vegetables: "She either harvested greens from meadows all day, or kneaded, sieved, wove till nightfall." (Chortatsis, "Panoria").

No other flora on earth has been investigated so thoroughly as the flora of the island of Crete. It all started in 15th century when a large number of botanists, pharmacologists, historians and travelers arrived on the island of Crete for a thorough examination of the local flora. French botanist Piere Belon recorded 96 plant species in their original, local names.

By order of the king of France Luis XIVI, French traveler-researcher Tournefort traveled east and came to Crete where he recorded 396 plant species. In 1794 one more French traveler, Olivier, arrived on Crete to report, in fascination, that the Cretans used the chickpea's leaves raw in salads and fried the leaves of beans stalks in olive oil.

Dutch physician Dapper, who visited Crete in 17th century, reported a wide range of edible herbs, greens and vegetables, among them the dittany (dictamus) which was also chewed by goats to heal their wounds.

THE NUTRITIONAL VALUE OF WILD GREENS – HERBS AND FRUIT THE MEDITERRANEAN DIET

In 1999 the National Centre for Nutrition, of the National School for Public Health, headed by Mrs. Antonia Trichopoulou, in collaboration with the General State Laboratory and the company Research and Technological Food Development (ETAT.S.A.) conducted a large scale research concerning the nutritional value of a group of 17 different wild herbs which were used in cottage pie recipes.

Scientific examination of Cretan pies confirmed the existence of flavonoids, substances of plant origin containing flavone in various combinations (anthoxanthins, apigenins, flavones, quercitins, etc.) and with varying biological activities. These substances are antioxidant and found in fruits and vegetables. Medical research on flavonoids has proven their positive action

in preventing cardiovascular diseases and tumor growths. The raw herbs or greens used in Cretan pies are rich in flavonoids while significant amounts are retained even after the pies are cooked. Herbs and greens rich in flavonoids are: the fennel, leek, poppy flower, sorrel and wild carrot.

The green parts of dandelions are rich in vitamin A. The nettle is a significant source of iron and carotene B. The chicory is rich in vitamin B12, which is necessary for cell function. The seeds of the wild rosebush are rich in vitamin C and the carob-beans in proteins. The mint and thyme are characterised by anticeptic and anti-microbial qualities, while the sage is used to heal wounds of the oral cavity. The chemical constitution of grapes is similar to mother's milk while the consumption of a glass of red wine protects the arteries of the heart. The fruits provide ample vegetable fibers and minerals which aid the function of the intestines.

EIGHT BASIC POINTS OF THE MEDITERRANEAN DIET

1. High ratio of monounsaturates (olive oil) over saturated lipids (butter, lard).
2. Moderate consumption of alcohol (1-2 glasses of red wine / day)
3. Large consumption of greens / vegetables.
4. Large consumption of cereals (including whole grain bread)
5. Large consumption of fruits.
6. Large consumption of herbs
7. Low consumption of meat and related products
8. Low consumption of milk and dairy products.

Individuals who abide by the above eight points are considered to be proportionally closer to the Mediterranean diet and a healthier living.

THE ANTIOXIDANT QUALITIES
OF HERBS
– OLIVE OIL WITH HERBS –

Vegetable oils scented with herbs and spices were extensively used in antiquity, but we have no knowledge of their application in the kitchen. We do know, however, that owing to their inherent qualities, vegetable oils were used for body care. Selected herbs were added to vegetable oils to lend them valuable curative, styptic and antioxidant qualities.

During the reign of Byzantine emperor Constantine "the purple-born", legist Cassianos Vassos is credited with a number of recipes for scented olive oil. Some of these recipes provide instructions for improving medium and low quality olive oils with the addition of aromatic herbs. For example, rancid olive oil improves with the addition of dill and foul-smelling olive oil with the addition of coriander or raisins. A popular practice in the villages of the province of Pediada, Crete, was to add 2-3 oregano sprigs in the large earthenware jars used as olive oil containers.

There has been a lot of research in the plant kingdom for substances with antioxidant qualities, particularly in herbs and aromatic plants, the main sources of antioxidants. Independent investigation results concur on the significant antioxidant qualities of the rosemary and oregano.

In 1952 Chipault noted that consumption of salted meat should be combined with infusions of rosemary, sage, and thyme. In addition, he claims that oregano in mayonnaise offers excellent antioxidant qualities.

Modern research is under way by the Aristotelian University with regard to the stability of olive oils mixed with rosemary, oregano, garlic and thyme.

THE PYRAMID OF THE MEDITERRANEAN DIET

1. Meat

2. Sweets

3. Eggs

4. Potatoes

5. Beans, Legumes and dried fruit

6. Poultry

7. Fish

8. Dairy

9. Olive oil and olives

10. Greens/Vegetables/Herbs/ Fruit

11. Pasta, Rice

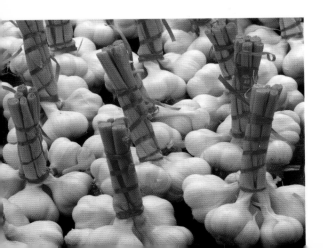

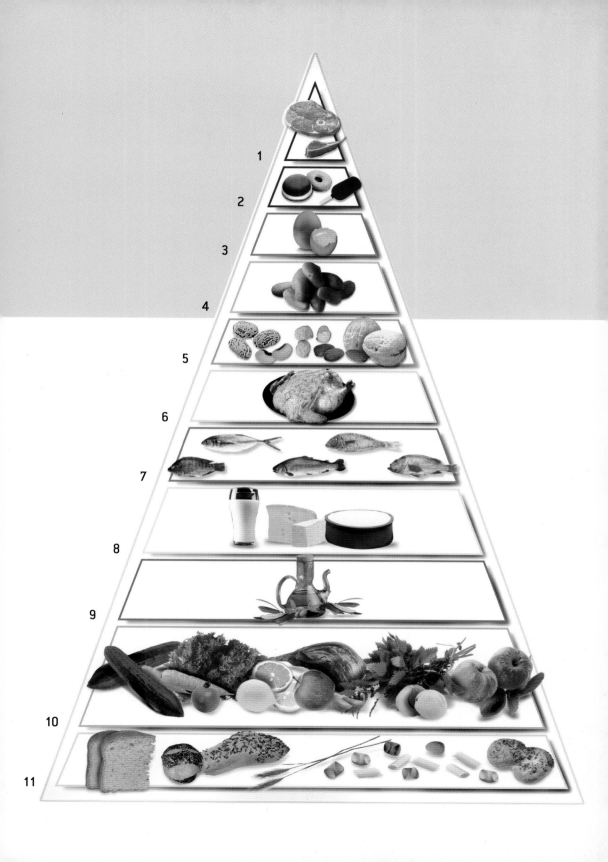

Wild greens

The seemingly bare hills and mountains of Crete, the rocky terrain, the thick olive groves, the deceptively barren fields, even the jugged shoreline of the island constitute the wider context where a very interesting flora thrives. This flora, an evolutionary link between the flora of Asia and Africa and that of Europe, offers a wide range of endemic plants. Most of these plants find numerous culinary applications around the island: they are consumed raw in salads; boiled with legumes, meat and fish, or used as basic ingredients in pies. According to estimates, approximately 100 different species of wild greens are edible on the island.

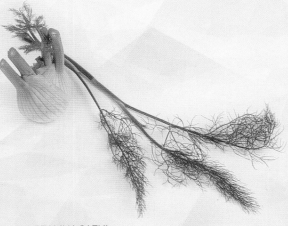

MARATHO
(Foeniculum vulgare Fennel):
The fennel has been known and used by the ancient Egyptians, Greeks, and Romans. Since then it occupies a prominent place among the cosmopolitan aromatic herbs in international gastronomy. The fennel enjoys wide culinary applications on Crete and mainland Greece. You can find it in cottage pies, mixed with octopus, cuttlefish, fish, snails, while it also marries well with legumes (e.g. black-eyed beans, broadbeans) and fresh vegetables (fresh beans and artichokes).

STAMNAGATHI
(Chichorium Intybus Chicory):
The most favourite herbaceous plant in Crete. It usually grows around the coastline of the island. Its taste is sub-bitter and consumed raw in salads (with the addition of olive oil and vinegar) and is also cooked with goat's meat in eggs & lemon sauces.

ASKOLIBRI
(Scolymus Salsify):
This is a thistle species whose edible parts are the tender leaves and the underground white and thick roots. The askolibri are delicious with goat's meat in egg & lemon sauce.

RADIKIA
(Cichorium Chicory):

This is one of the most favourite greens in the broader region of the Mediterranean basin. It can be consumed in large quantities either raw, in salads, or cooked. It is an excellent tonic for the human body.

The roots, tender leaves and shoots are served cooked or raw with a lot of olive oil and vinegar or lemon juice. The sweet chicory variety is cooked with meat. A delicious Cretan salad includes chicory as main ingredient accompanied with other sweet or aromatic herbs/greens.

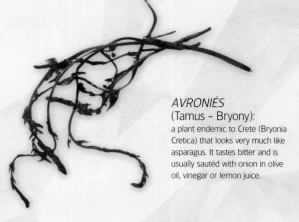

AVRONIÉS
(Tamus – Bryony):

a plant endemic to Crete (Bryonia Cretica) that looks very much like asparagus. It tastes bitter and is usually sautéd with onion in olive oil, vinegar or lemon juice.

STIFNOS
(Solanum – Black nightshade):

This is a small weed that grows in the summer months. In many parts of Greece the Stifnos is considered poisonous. However, on Crete it is consumed in large quantities either boiled or mixed with other blites and courgettes.

ASKORDOULAKI
(Muscari Comosum – Tassel Hyacinth):

actually, the edible parts of this plant are the underground bulbs. They are delicious! However, before they are ready for consumption you will have to soak them in water for some time. The Cretan bulbs are used in salads or cooked with lamb in the villages of the Rethymnon prefecture. If you would like to taste them, look for salads or meat dishes with Askordoulàki in their ingredients, or inquire in restaurants.

GLISTRIDA
(Portulaca oleracea – Purslane):

This is a weed with thick, succulent and fleshy leaves with smooth margins. It is a precious ingredient for Cretan salads and is also boiled in a casserole with fish or meat.

PAPOÚLES
(Pisum Sativum – Garden pea):

a pea species whose edible parts are the flat, tender tops. They are consumed raw in salads. In local dialect the papoùles are also known as 'psarés' or 'kabliés.'

SMOKED PORK WITH 3 HERBS

Serves 8

INGREDIENTS

1 pork shoulder with bone, 2 kg

1 bunch of dried oregano

1 bunch of dried sage

1 bunch of dried thyme

lemon leaves

salt

DIRECTIONS

1. Roughly cut the pork shoulder into slices and sprinkle with salt. Let them rest for 8-10 hours. Subsequently, arrange the pieces on grill in the oven and place below the grill a baking pan with water to catch the melting fat. Grill at 200°C for 30 minutes, then lower heat at 180°C and continue grilling for at least one hour and ten minutes.

2. When the pork slices are golden brown, remove the baking pan below the grill and carefully dispose of its contents. Place the chopped herbs in a fire-proof earthenware in the place of the baking pan and light up the herbs with a match (turn off the main power switch first). Let them burn for 1-2 minutes, then blow fire out. The smoke emitted will provide an excellent scent to the pork slices.

3. On a flat surface arrange side-by-side 2-3 baking sheets, spread the lemon leaves and the hot pork slices on top of them. Wrap the meat pieces well and let cool off for 1 hour. Serve with ample salad.

LARGE, LIMA BEANS WITH SAGE

Serves 6

INGREDIENTS

500 gr large lima beans

6 cups of cold water

1/4 cup extra virgin olive oil

1 1/2 tbsp sage, finely chopped

1 large clove garlic, crushed

DIRECTIONS

1. Place the beans in a large pot. Add cold water to top beans by approximately 3 inches and let them soak overnight.

2. Strain the beans and place them back into the pot. Add the 6 cups of cold water, 1/4 cup of olive oil, sage (finely chopped) and garlic. Place the pot on oven ring at high temperature. On first boil, lower the temperature to moderate reading.

3. Cover the pot with lid and simmer for 45 min. or until the beans are tender. Occasionally stir the beans. Then strain the beans and sprinkle with the salt and pepper.

4. With a strainer–ladle transfer the beans to a bowl. Pour the olive oil over the beans and garnish with fresh sage.

FRIED SAGE LEAVES
Serves 10

INGREDIENTS
The Batter
1 egg, the yolk
350 ml very chilled water
1/8 tsp soda
185 gr all purpose flour
30 large sage leaves

DIRECTIONS

In a large metallic bowl mix all of the above ingredients, excepting the
sage. Gently stir the ingredients with a wooden spoon to a watery mixture.
Since this mixture looses its texture fast, pick the sage leaves and dip
them in the batter and then into the frying pan with hot corn oil. This
should not take more than 10 minutes. While frying, decide when the
sage leaves are crispy enough to remove.

PORK LIVER WITH SAGE
Serves 6

INGREDIENTS
1kg pork liver, chopped (small pieces)
1 1/2 cups olive oil
1 cup flour, hard
3-4 sage leaves (dry or fresh)
1/2 tablespoons vinegar, strong (from red wine)
salt to taste

DIRECTIONS

1. Wash the liver well under tap water, pat it dry with kitchen paper and chop it. Roll the lives cuts
over a thin layer of flour. Do not salt them. Brown the liver in hot oil until a crust forms on them.
2. Add the sage, season with salt, stir and pour the vinegar over all cuts. Let the liver boil in its
sauce for 3-4 minutes. Serve the liver warm in its sauce.

PASTRIES WITH CHEESE AND SAFFRON

INGREDIENTS

240 gr. butter milk

160 gr granulated sugar

2 eggs

4 cups flour

Filling:

1 kg ricotta or other sweet and soft cheese

2-3 saffron stamens, dissolved in slightly warm water

1 egg

3 tbsp granulated sugar

1 egg yolk (for brushing)

cinnamon

DIRECTIONS

1. In a mixer process the butter, milk and sugar at medium speed for 3 minutes. Slowly add the eggs and flour until the mixture turns into a very soft dough. Slightly butter a few moulds (4cm high) and line them with the dough.

2. Fill the moulds with the mixture of sweet cheese. Brush the top of the mixture with the egg yolk, dust with a little cinnamon and bake in preheated oven at 180ºC for 30 minutes.

3. Let the cakes cool and then remove the moulds. Serve cakes cool.

"*KARTERAKI*" DRINK
(HERBAL BLEND TEA)

INGREDIENTS

1/2 tsp sage

1 tsp marjoram

1 tsp dictamus

1/2 tsp chamomile

DIRECTIONS

1. Mix the herbs in a bowl.

2. Soak them in 4 cups of warm (70ºC) water. Cover the bowl with a flat dish and let the drink rest for 10 minutes. Strain and serve immediately.

PUNCH

INGREDIENTS

1 tablespoon sage

2 tablespoons grape juice syrup

3/4 cup rice

400 ml water

black pepper (5 whole grains)

DIRECTIONS

1. Bring water to a boil in a pot and add the sage and pepper seeds. Cover the pot and let the sage boil for 3 minutes.

2. Remove pot from the oven ring; let pot stand covered aside for 5 minutes and then strain over another pot.

3. Add the raki and grape juice syrup into the bowl. Stir very well to mix the ingredients and heat for 3 minutes. Serve warm in winter.

GREEN SALAD WITH POMEGRANATE AND HERBS

Serves 6

INGREDIENTS

1/2 chicory, finely chopped

2 cups endives, finely chopped

2 spring onions, finely chopped

2 tablespoons olive oil

1 level teaspoon oregano

1 teaspoon vinegar

4 tablespoons pomegranate seeds

salt to taste

DIRECTIONS

1. Remove brown or dry leaves from the greens and rinse them under tap water well. Strain and chop the greens finely, and toss them in a bowl.

2. Pour in the olive oil little by little, the oregano and sprinkle the salt over the greens. Spread the pomegranate seeds over and sprinkle the salad with a little vinegar. Serve!

FRESH COURGETTES SALAD

Serves 6

INGREDIENTS

2 cups thinly grated courgettes

1 cup fresh yogurt

2 tablespoons lemon juice

2 cloves garlic, mashed

1 teaspoon dill, finely chopped

salt & pepper to taste

DIRECTIONS

Mix all of the ingredients in a bowl. Refrigerate the bowl for 2–3 hours. Serve cold with ample dill for garnish.

INGREDIENTS

2 eggs, boiled and cut to four slices

3 fresh artichokes, the hearts

1 cup broad beans, fresh and shelled

1 spring onion

a few Kalamata olives

salt to taste

1 tablespoon olive oil

1 teaspoon vinegar

1 large lemon, the juice of

1 tablespoon flour

ARTICHOKES SALAD

Serves 6

DIRECTIONS

1. If you purchase the artichokes from the greengrocer or the market, remove the outer leaves until you get to the tender leaves. Chop away the tapering, thorny portion (approx. half way between the tip and the meat of the artichoke) and use a knife to peel away any green skin around the heart, so that you get only the meat (heart) of the artichoke. Alternatively, purchase artichoke hearts from the supermarket. Toss the hearts into a bowl of water where you have previously dissolved the flour and the lemon juice. Slice each heart in half, remove fuzz, and chop further to thinner slices. Toss slices into a large salad bowl then add the broad beans, eggs, coarsely chopped onion and olives; sprinkle with the salt; pour in the olive oil and vinegar and stir to mix well. Serve immediately.

TZATZIKI WITH CUCUMBER

Serves 6

INGREDIENTS

2 medium size cucumbers, do not peel

2 cloves garlic, mashed

4 tablespoons olive oil

1 tablespoon vinegar, strong

2 1/2 cups yogurt, strained

1 teaspoon salt

DIRECTIONS

1. Finely grate the cucumbers over a bowl and sprinkle with the salt. Pick handfuls from the grated cucumber and squeeze them between your hands to let their water out, which you dispose in the kitchen sink.

2. Place the yogurt, garlic, olive oil and vinegar in a bowl and beat them with a fork (or blend) for 2–3 minutes to mix the ingredients well. Then add the grated cucumber and stir vigorously with a fork (or blend). Transfer the tzatziki to small bowls and refrigerate for half an hour. The *tzatziki* is meant to be a dip for stuffed vine leaves or sauce for pitas. Best served cold.

"HARVEST" SALAD – PURSLANE & POTATOES

Serves 6

INGREDIENTS

2 cups coarsely chopped purslane

2 large potatoes, boiled and cubed

1 cucumber, cubed

1 large tomato, sliced

1 large onion, cut to rings

1 tablespoon dill, finely chopped

2 eggs, boiled and cut to four slices

2-3 tablespoons olive oil

2 tablespoons vinegar

salt to taste

DIRECTIONS

1. Boil the potatoes, let them cool down and cube them. Mix the potatoes with the purslane in a bowl. Add a little salt, the onion, tomato, cucumber, olive oil and the vinegar.

2. Use two spoons to shuffle (toss up) the salad and add a little more salt. Garnish with the eggs and dill. Serve at room temperature.

"DAKOS": RUSK WITH TOMATO, FETA CHEESE AND OREGANO

Serves 4

INGREDIENTS

4 round barley rusks
2 tomatoes, large and ripe
3-4 tablespoons olive oil
2 tablespoons grated feta cheese
1/2 teaspoon oregano
salt to taste

DIRECTIONS

1. Run the barley rusks under tap water to wet the top side a little. Roughly chop or grate the tomatoes over the top.

2. Sprinkle the barley rusks with half of the olive quantity and with a little salt. Spread the grated tomato on top and sprinkle with the grated *feta* cheese or *myzithra*.

3. Next, sprinkle with salt and oregano and pour the remaining olive oil on top.

FISH ROE SALAD *TARAMOSALATA*
Served in 2 little bowls

INGREDIENTS

2 tablespoons roe (white or red)

1/2 bread (the crumbs)

3/4 cup virgin olive oil

1 clove garlic

1 lemon, the juice of

DIRECTIONS

Soak the breadcrumbs in water and squeeze them in your hands to strain water completely. Put the crumbs in a blender, add the garlic cloves, the roe and start blending the mixture at medium speed. Add the olive oil and lemon juice little by little, alternating between the two, to get a homogenous thin paste. Serve in two little bowls.

CASSEROLE CELERY
Serves 6

INGREDIENTS

3 pieces of celery, medium-sized, only the roots cut to half

3 medium-sized carrots, cubed

10-12 onions, small

1/2 teaspoon sugar

1 teaspoon salt

6 tablespoons lemon juice

1/2 water glass virgin olive oil

2-2 1/2 glasses lukewarm water

DIRECTIONS

1. Clean the celery and remove their hard or dry parts. Slice them along their length so that you get two longitudinal pieces, each bearing a groove from one end to another. Then cut each piece in half.

2. Place the celery pieces in a casserole along with the carrots, onions, olive oil and water. Add the salt, lemon juice and sugar. Place the casserole over high heat and cook for 20-25 minutes, until all water in the casserole is absorbed by the ingredients. Turn off heat and serve at room temperature.

STUFFED ARTICHOKES WITH YOGURT SAUCE AND MINT

Serves 6

INGREDIENTS

6 artichoke heads, fresh/canned/frozen

4 tbsp rice (used in stuffed vegetables)

1 1/2 tbsp mint, finely chopped

3 spring onions, finely chopped

1 medium size onion bulb, finely ground

1 tbsp white wine, unresinated

7 tbsp yogurt (strained)

1 large egg

lemon juice, from a large lemon

1 cup olive oil

salt

green pepper, freshly ground

DIRECTIONS

1. In a small saucepan heat the olive oil and sauté the spring onion for 2–3 minutes. Stir in the rice and add the wine. Add three tablespoons of water, cover the pan and simmer for 7 minutes. Stir in half the mint then turn off oven ring leaving the saucepan on to simmer for a while.

2. Peel the artichokes down to the very tender leaves. Crew-cut the remaining leaves and using a pointed knife remove the little mauve leaves and fuzz from the heart of the artichokes to form a cavity. Toss the artichokes in a bowl with water where you have previously added the lemon juice and a teaspoon of salt.

3. Pull each artichoke out of the bowl, and rub them all over with a lemon cut in half. Fill each artichoke cavity with the mixture of rice.

4. Heat 1/2 cup of olive oil in a casserole and sauté the ground onion until it releases its juice, without getting brown. Place the artichokes in circular fashion at the bottom of the casserole, add a cup of water, cover and simmer for 12 minutes.

5. Transfer the artichokes with their juice to a small pyrex dish. Take a bowl and whisk the yogurt with the egg and a lot of green pepper. Pour this sauce over the artichokes and then cook in a preheated oven at 180ºC for 30 minutes.

6. Serve the artichokes hot with their sauce. Sprinkle with a lot of mint.

STUFFED VINE LEAVES WITH MINCED MEAT IN *AVGOLEMONO*

Serves 8-10

INGREDIENTS

600gr vine leaves

1kg minced meat

1/2 water glass rice

1/2 cup parsley, finely chopped

1 tablespoon mint, finely chopped

3 large onions, finely chopped

1 water glass olive oil

1 1/2 water glasses lukewarm water

1/2 teaspoon salt

1/2 teaspoon cumin

1/2 teaspoon pepper

Avgolemono (eggs & lemon sauce)

2 tablespoons corn flour or rice flour

2 tablespoons lemon juice

2 eggs, the yolks

salt and pepper to taste

DIRECTIONS

1. If the vine leaves are fresh, blanch them in boiling water for 2-3 minutes and remove their stems. If the vine leaves are canned, rinse them under tap water only.

2. Mix the minced meat with the rice, parsley, mint, onions and cumin. Season the mixture with the salt and pepper.

3. Place a tablespoon of filling near the stem end, roll once and fold the sides in. Repeat the rolling and folding of sides until you have reached the end of the leaf. The final product is a stuffed vine leaf, a roll of about 1 1/2 -2 inches long. Repeat the process with the remaining leaves, but keep some leaves for lining the bottom of a pot. We usually keep those leaves that are either shredded or not so convenient for stuffing.

4. Place the stuffed vine leaves on top of the lining in the pot and pour one glass of olive oil and 1/2 glass of lukewarm water over them and cover with a dish to secure them in place. Place the pot over medium heat. You may need to add a little water during the cooking process.

5. Next, prepare the eggs & lemon sauce (*avgolemono*): in a bowl whisk the yolks and gradually add the lemon juice whisking at the same time. Using a ladle pick some stock from the pot and whisk it in the bowl with the eggs and lemon. Dissolve the corn flour in a little cold water and mix it with the sauce in a pan. Season the mixture with salt and pepper and bring it to a boil over medium heat. This sauce looks like a thin cream.

6. When the stuffed vine leaves are done (taste one to see if the rice is done), place them carefully in a large serving plate and the sauce in a bowl. Individual portions are served in standard deep dishes with the sauce spread all over them using a table spoon or small ladle.

INGREDIENTS

1 large and soft white cabbage
500gr minced beef or a
mixture of beef and pork
3 onions, medium-sized and
chopped
1 cup rice (not full to the brim)
3 tablespoons parsley, finely
chopped
1 tablespoon dill, finely
chopped
1 glass olive oil

3 glasses of water
1/2 teaspoon cumin
1/2 teaspoon salt
1/2 teaspoon pepper

For the Egg and Lemon Sauce:
2 eggs
3 lemons, the juice of
2 level tablespoons corn flour
or rice flour

STUFFED CABBAGE
Serves 8-10

DIRECTIONS

1. Mix the minced meat with the rice, onion, parsley and dill. Season the mixture with the salt and pepper and let it stand aside.

2. Blanch the cabbage in boiling water with its core at the bottom of the pot, until the leaves are just soft. Remove the blanched cabbage from the pot. If the stem is too thick, cut core in small pieces like a chopped onion. Peel the leaves carefully off the cabbage; it may still be burning hot.

3. Arrange the leaves on the kitchen bench or large tray. Pick a cabbage leaf, place it on a wooden board or smaller tray and sliver a portion of its hard vein (if any) to thin it out. Stuff each leaf with the filling mixture. Starting at the bottom of the leaf, roll up one turn, then turn in the sides of the leaf to cover the filling, then roll up some more until you reach the top of the leaf to make a little bundle or cylinder. Place the bundle in a crock pot and repeat the procedure with the remaining leaves.

4. Before you place your first bundle in the crock pot, line the bottom of the pot with blanched cabbage leaves and place the bundles on top of them. When you have exhausted all cabbage leaves, sprinkle the bundles with olive oil, salt, pepper, 3 glasses of water. You may cover the bundles in the pot with a dish to keep them in place. Cook over moderate heat for 60-90 minutes.

5. When the stuffed cabbage leaves are almost done, prepare the egg & lemon sauce by whisking the eggs with the lemon juice and corn flour. Remove the pot from the ring and use a ladle to take out a generous amount of stock from the pot and whisk it in your eggs & lemon sauce. Pour this sauce over the stuffed leaves and shake the pot by the handles to allow the sauce to settle into the pot.

6. Boil the stuffed cabbage leaves for 3 more minutes, for the corn flour to dissolve well. Serve warm or at room temperature.

CASSEROLE AUBERGINES STUFFED WITH CHEESE

Serves 6

INGREDIENTS

6 aubergines, elongated variety

1/4 kefalotyri cheese (a type of hard cheese),
  cut to 6 thin and long pieces

2 large tomatoes, mashed

2 onions, finely chopped

8 cloves garlic, finely chopped

2 cups olive oil

2 teaspoons salt

pepper

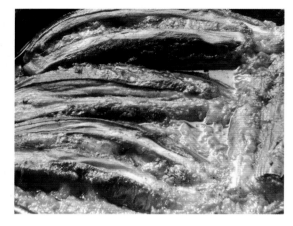

INGREDIENTS

1. Wash the aubergines, remove their stems and place them in salted water to 'sweeten' them a little.

2. Slice them in half lengthwise and scoop out the pulp with a teaspoon, being careful not to damage the skin. Season them with salt and fill each 'trough' with a piece of cheese and a little from the finely chopped garlic and onion.

3. Use a pot to sauté half the onion in olive oil for five minutes and arrange the aubergines next to each other in the pot.

4. Top them with the mashed tomato, add a large glass of water and let the meal cook on low heat (100ºC) without stirring. When the meal is done, serve and sprinkle each serving with grated cheese (kefalotyri).

CAULIFLOWER STEW

Serves 6

INGREDIENTS

1 kg cauliflower

2 large tomatoes, mashed

1/2 teaspoon tomato paste

1 large onion, finely chopped

1/2 bunch parsley

3/4 cup olive oil

3 Guinea grains

1 cinnamon stick

salt to taste

freshly ground pepper to taste

DIRECTIONS

1. Wash the cauliflower and peel away the dry or withered parts, but keep all the tender parts.

2. Use a stew pot to sauté the onion for 4-5 minutes, then add the cauliflower and 1 cup of water.

3. Cover the pot and boil the cauliflower for 10 minutes over strong heat.

4. Add the tomatoes, parsley, all spices and 1 cup water. Continue boiling until the cauliflower is tender enough.

5. Remove the cinnamon stick and serve the meal warm or lukewarm in its sauce.

ARTICHOKES WITH DILL IN OLIVE OIL

Serves 6

INGREDIENTS

6-7 artichokes

2 large potatoes, cut to four pieces each

2 carrots, sliced

1 tablespoon dill, finely chopped

2 spring onions, finely chopped

1/2 cup olive oil

1 large lemon, the juice of

1 teaspoon flour

salt and pepper to taste

DIRECTIONS

1. Use a pot to sauté the spring onions lightly and add the meat of the artichokes cut in half, the potatoes, dill and two cups of water. Cover the pot and simmer for 12 minutes. Remove the lid and continue cooking for 12 more minutes.

2. Dissolve the flour in the lemon juice and season the mixture with salt and pepper. Add this mixture to the pot and continue simmering for 2–3 minutes. Serve the artichokes warm or at room temperature.

STUFFED MARROWS WITH *AVGOLEMONO*

Serves 6

INGREDIENTS

10 medium-sized marrows

3 tablespoons rice

1/2 kg minced meat, beef

1 medium-sized onion, grated

1 tablespoon dill, finely

chopped

1 teaspoon salt

1/2 teaspoon pepper

1/2 teaspoon cumin

1/2 cup olive oil

Sauce:

1 egg

1 lemon, the juice of

salt

DIRECTIONS

1. Cut the marrows 2 cm below the stem end, but keep the cut end for plug. Pick a dessert spoon to deseed the marrows by scooping out their pulp and fill them in with a mixture of minced meat, rice, onion, dill, salt, pepper and cumin. Plug each marrow with the stem-end previously removed. Place the marrow into a pot.

2. Pour the olive oil and one cup of water into the pot, cover with the lid and simmer the marrows for 25–30 minutes. Turn off heat and let pot on the ring for 10 more minutes. In the meanwhile, prepare the sauce: use a bowl to whisk the egg pouring the lemon juice in small quantities and a little stock from the pot. This is your *avgolemono* sauce. Pour the *avgolemono* sauce over the meal in the pot and serve 10 minutes later.

PANCAKES WITH COURGETTES

Serves 6-8

INGREDIENTS

3 cups water

1/4 kg hard feta cheese

1-2 tomatoes, skinned and finely chopped

2 medium-sized courgettes, grated–seasoned and drained

1 medium-sized onion, finely chopped

2 eggs

1 bunch parsley, finely chopped

salt and pepper to taste

flour (as much as its takes to get thin mash)

olive oil for frying

DIRECTIONS

1. Mix all solid ingredients into a bowl. Add the water and mash the ingredients using a fork.

2. Heat the olive oil in a skillet and spoon in small 'islands' from the mixture into the bowl. Approximately one level tablespoon will be enough per 'island' of mixture.

3. Fry the pancakes on both sides until golden brown. When done, use a perforated spoon to transfer the pancakes onto a large plate lined with kitchen paper. Serve the pancakes when they are crispy enough.

VEGETABLES STUFFED WITH RICE AND FENNEL

Serves 6

INGREDIENTS

2 large and ripe tomatoes

2 courgettes

2 aubergines

2 green sweet peppers

8 cups rice

4 onions, large & finely chopped

5 fennel roots

1 carrot, grated

1 artichoke heart, grated

1 courgette, grated

the pulp from one tomato

6 tablespoons olive oil (for the filling)

2 tablespoons olive oil (for cooking)

1 teaspoon sugar

1/2 teaspoon oregano

salt and pepper to taste

DIRECTIONS

1. Wash all vegetables and cut off their tops to deseed them using a dessert spoon, making sure not to damage their skin. Mix the vegetables pulp, finely chop it and place it in a bowl. Sprinkle the pulp with salt and set it aside. Season the hollows of the deseeded vegetables with salt and turn them upside down to drain their juices.

2. Choose a large bowl to pour in the olive oil (6 tablespoons), the pulp from the deseeded vegetables, the chopped onions, carrots, artichoke hearts, courgettes, fennel, and the rice, spices, sugar and salt.

3. Use your hands to mix all the ingredients in the bowl. Stuff the vegetables with this mixture and seal them with the tops you have kept.

4. Arrange the stuffed vegetables in a baking pan and grate a ripe tomato over them. Pour in the olive oil (1 cup), cover the pan with foil and cook in the oven at 150ºC for half an hour. Remove the foil at half the cooking period and allow the stuffed vegetables to brown a little. Serve warm.

NETTLE SPIRAL PIES

20 pies

INGREDIENTS

1 kg nettles

3 spring onions

1/2 cup black vinegary olive oils, deseeded and finely chopped

1/2 cup walnuts, crushed

4 cups olive oil (for frying)

little cumin

salt

pepper

for the pastry sheet:

2 cups flour

1 tbsp vodka

4 tbsp olive oil

1 cup lukewarm water

salt

DIRECTIONS

1. Clean and rinse the nettles well under running water.

2. Strain the nettles well and sauté them in a deep pan with the onions in 5 tablespoons of olive oil for 5 minutes. Add the olives, walnuts, cumin, salt and pepper. Test to see if the cumin and pepper are to your liking. Add more if required.

3. Pastry sheet preparation: mix the vodka with olive oil, salt, a little flour and a little lukewarm water. Process at low speed for 10 minutes and gradually add the flour. Occasionally stop processing to check if the dough holds together. If the dough is runny, add a little flour, then check again. Stop processing if the dough is to your satisfaction.

4. On a slightly floured board roll out the dough and cut in rectangular strips of 7 cm wide and 30 cm long. Spoon in a little of the filling along each strip and bring the long sides together to close the strips. Hold one end of the filled strip and roll it in to form a spiral.

5. Preheat ample olive oil in a frying pan and fry the nettle pies. Serve them warm.

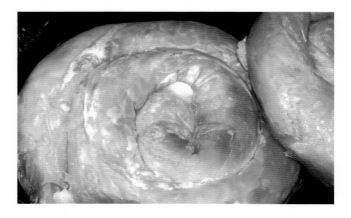

RABBIT FRICASSEE WITH CHICORY
Serves 6

INGREDIENTS

1 rabbit, medium-sized

1kg chicory (sweet) or endives

1 cup olive oil

2 onions

2 eggs

1 lemon, the juice of

salt and pepper to taste

DIRECTIONS

1. Wash the rabbit and cut it to pieces. Use a deep pot to brown the rabbit pieces in olive oil and chopped onion.

2. Add 1 1/2 cups of water and the salt; cover the pot and cook at 180ºC for 20 minutes. Add the chicory (cut them in half if long), two cups of water and let the meal simmer at 150ºC for 25 minutes.

3. Whisk the eggs adding the lemon juice gradually and do the same with stock from the pot. Remove the pot from the oven ring and let the meal stand for 6 minutes before you pour in the eggs and lemon sauce. Serve warm.

CHICORY WITH LAMB AND CORIANDER
Serves 6

INGREDIENTS

1 kg wild chicory, finely chopped

1 kg lamb (shoulder blade) in pieces

2 onions, finely sliced

2 large ripe tomatoes, finely chopped

3/4 cup olive oil

1 tsp dried coriander

4 seeds of pimento

salt

pepper, freshly ground (as much as you prefer)

DIRECTIONS

1. Stir-fry the onions in the olive oil until slightly roasted. Add the meat in slices. Continue stir-frying until the lamb pieces acquire a golden-brown colour. Add the salt, coriander, pimento and two cups of water. Stir well and cover the container to simmer for 40 minutes approximately.

2. Pick a little meat with fork to taste it. When meat is almost done, add the chicory, tomatoes, a little water and stir. Continue cooking for 20-30 more minutes.

3. Sprinkle with freshly ground pepper and serve while the meal is still warm.

"Pork is the meat of choice at Christmas in Crete. The image of pork in a large platter - plum, crispy skin and fragrant - is incontestable. The sheer size of it in relation to chicken - the garnish and its taste are magnificent!"

Pork

An extract from a Greek playwright, Antiphanes (388–311 BC), informs us that the ancient Greeks sacrificed piglets to honour goddess Athena (Venus). During the Greek–Roman period ancient Greek farmers also sacrificed pigs in festivals honouring Cronus and Demeter in supplication of a rich crop.

The modern "sacrifice" of pigs / piglets and the carving of pork at Christmas in Crete are part and parcel with a ritual aiming to lustrate the home and the family from all evil influences. From a psychological point of view, lustration is achieved with the flowing of the blood of pigs/piglets. Besides the cultural and ritual aspect involving this animal, the most interesting part relates to the way people preserve the entire pig or piglet for culinary applications. Pork is the meat of choice at Christmas in Crete. The image of pork in a large platter — plum, crispy skin and fragrant — is incontestable. The sheer size of it — in relation to chicken — the garnish and its taste are magnificent!

The legs and griskin were usually reserved for making apaki (smoked pork). Tender saddle cuts are usually baked in the oven and served with potatoes in lemon juice, or cooked with leeks and celery. The intestines are thoroughly cleaned and stuffed (sausage) with finely chopped meat or finely chopped liver and rice (*omathies*). The fat was heated and mixed with smoked pork pieces to make delicious syglina and crunchy *tsigarides*.

PORK JELLY (*PECHTY*)

As soon as the pig is slaughtered the Cretans boil its head and feet immediately. It takes a few hours to convert these items into a translucent, refreshing and spicy dish: the local tsiladia (or *pechty* or *zeladia* or *zalatina*).

This delicacy — known by its Venetian name, tsiladia, – is prepared in Crete on the day following Christmas Day (26 December) and consumed on New Year's Day. The ingredients are simple: in addition to the meat, you will need a lot of bigarade juice, bay leaves and cumin.

OMATHIES or HEMATIES

This rather "strange" way to prepare sausages (omathies) is rare in Crete today. However, according to ancient sources, the sausages produced were famous during the Byzantine period. The traditional way of making omathies at Christmas was practiced in various parts of Greece (Crete, Corfu and Peloponnese) until the early 20th century. The recipe involved finely chopped pork meat, oatmeal/gruel or rice and a little blood from the animal (pig). During the last few decades the recipe for omathies involved the following: pork intestines stuffed with gruel/oatmeal, blanched almonds, herbs, cinnamon and pepper.

SAUSAGES

The sausages made in Crete are stuffed with chopped pork and smoked over burning sage sprigs and cypress tree branches. They taste delicious with strong vinegar and cumin.

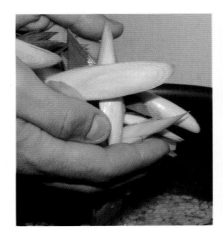

PORK WITH LEEKS
Serves 6

INGREDIENTS

1kg pork, cubed

1kg leeks, chopped to 4-5 cm long

2-3 tomatoes, peeled and mashed

3/4 cup olive oil

1/2 cup red wine

salt, pepper

1 medium-sized lemon, the juice

DIRECTIONS

1. In a pot heat the olive oil to sauté the pork until lightly brown on all sides. Then pour in the wine and let the pot on the heat for 2-3 more minutes until the wine has evaporated.

2. Add the leeks, tomato and one and a half cups of water. Cover the pot and simmer for 30-45 minutes with the lid on. Taste and correct with a little salt, pepper and/or lemon.

TSILADIA

INGREDIENTS

The head of a medium-sized pig

5-6 pigs feet

1/2 kg meat (shoulder or neck)

1 cup bigarade juice

1 cup lemon juice

2 cups vinegar

2 slices of orange rind

1 teaspoon pepper

1 teaspoon cumin

1 tablespoon salt

2-3 bay leaves

DIRECTIONS

1. Clean and wash the head very well. Scorch any hairs on the feet using the flame of a candle, and then wash the feet. Use a large pot to boil the head, feet and meat for at least 2 hours. Skim out any froth that accumulates on the surface of the stock.

2. Transfer all the meat to a colander and let drain and cool down. Remove bones and slice all meat to small pieces.

3. Transfer the stock into a casserole and add the meat, bigarade juice, lemon, orange rind and half the spices. Boil them for 7-10 minutes with the casserole uncovered.

4. Let the stock stand for 7-10 minutes. Depending on the quantity of your stock, pick a number of small (clay) bowls and fill them with stock. Before you do that, sprinkle each bowl with cumin and pepper and place a bay leaf at the bottom, then pour the stock into the bowls. Let them stand for 24 hours for the stock to coagulate, then store in the fridge.

SIZZLED PORK or *FOUKAKI*

Serves 6

The classical and simple recipe for sizzled pork (tsitsiristo) follows. However, you can make adjustments, e.g. add one glass of wine and spices (cumin and chopped coriander)

INGREDIENTS

1kg pork (shoulder), cubed

1 cup olive oil

1 cup water

1 small lemon, the juice

pepper

DIRECTIONS

1. Use a heavy bottom casserole or large frying pan to add the meat, olive oil and water. Simmer for 20 minutes with casserole uncovered.

2. When the meat softens and is almost done, season with salt and raise temperature. Soon the water in the casserole will evaporate and the meat will cook in the oil.

3. When the meat starts to turn brown, transfer it on a platter using a perforated spoon and pour the lemon juice over it.

PORK WITH CELERY IN EGGS & LEMON SAUCE

Serves 6

INGREDIENTS

1kg pork (shoulder or neck)

2 onions, finely chopped

1 1/2 kg celery, root and leaves

3 tablespoons butter

2 eggs

2 lemons, the juice

salt & pepper

DIRECTIONS

1. Wash and slice meat to small pieces. Use a deep casserole to high heat butter and sauté the meat and onion. Then add water to the casserole, enough to cover the meat, and cook the meat until done.

2. In the meantime, wash and cut the celery to small pieces, boil it in salted water and then transfer it to a colander to drain.

3. Just before the meat is done, add to the celery, salt and pepper to the casserole and continue cooking. Make the eggs and lemon sauce. When the meat is done, remove casserole from heat and pour in the sauce (slowly, stirring at the same time). Serve warm.

PORK WITH CORIANDER

Serves 6

INGREDIENTS

1kg pork (shoulder / leg) cut to portions

1 cup red wine

1 tablespoon coriander, whole

1/2 cup olive oil

salt and pepper

DIRECTIONS

1. Sizzle the meat in olive oil until golden brown on all sides and then pour in the wine. Following, add 1/2 cup water and all the spices.

2. Cover the cooking vessel and simmer for 45-50 minutes.

3. Serve the meat warm in its sauce.

PORK w. QUINCE

Serves 8

INGREDIENTS

1/2 cup olive oil

1kg pork (shoulder or neck) cut to slices

1 tablespoon cloves

1 cup red wine

1 cinnamon stick

7 small onions

1 kg quinces

1 tablespoon (level) sugar or honey

DIRECTIONS

1. Heat 4-5 tablespoons of olive oil in a deep pan or shallow casserole and sauté the pork slices until brown on all sides. Then transfer the pork on a platter using a perforated spatula. Stick the cloves to the onions and place them into the casserole / pan with the olive oil.

2. Replace the pork into the casserole / pan and add the wine. Add the cinnamon and the salt. Cook over moderate heat for 5 minutes and then add one cup of water. Simmer the meal and onions for 30-40 min. with the casserole/pan covered, until the meat is half done. If you establish that the sauce is not enough, add a little water.

3. Wash, clean, quarter and deseed the quinces. Also, remove hard fiber from their core. Sauté the quinces in olive oil until golden brown on all sides.

4. Heat the oven at 180°C. Transfer the meat, quinces and onion into a pyrex dish or clay pot. Sprinkle the quinces with half the sugar quantity. Pour the sauce over the meal and sprinkle with the rest of sugar.

5. Cover the pyrex dish or clay pot with lid or aluminum foil and bake in the oven for 30-40 minutes. Occasionally, baste the meat and quinces with the sauce to keep them moist.
Serve warm.

"The *ofto* style of cooking meat is practiced in the country side, mainly by people living on mountainous regions. Alternatively, numerous recipes exist for cooking lamb or goat's meat in a wood-fired oven."

Lamb – Goat

COOKED AGAINST HEAT

The ofto style of cooking meat is an open air operation that lasts for approximately 5-6 hours. The requirements: goat's meat or lamb, dry and bare tree-branches, the right frame of mind. This is an age-old way of cooking meat which involves the digging of a small pit on the ground to accommodate the dry branches. If the live coals are a determining factor for the success of the meat on the spit, the direction of the wind is a determining factor for the success of the ofto meat. The 'chefs' skilled in this style of cooking are stern, composed and laconic in their answers. They wield the butcher's knife with artistry, severing half of the animal's torso in four large pieces to pierce each with a long spit of wood. The spits are resourced locally and spear-shaped by the 'chefs' themselves.

Next, the shepherds dig up a pit and, mindful of the direction of the wind, they stick the blunt ends of spits into the ground, at a distance that is just right for the heat to cook the meat pierced through the spits.

When the meat is cooked from one side, the 'chefs' do the necessary adjustments to the location of the spits. On this occasion, the women in attendance cut a few slices from the sides of the meat that is already done and serve it to the guests, with a salad on the side made from fresh, wild artichokes, fennel, dill, lettuce or with beetroot and *stamnagathi* (wild, bitter chicory). This style of cooking meat marries well with white and delicate sauces which include lemon juice.

The ofto style of cooking meat is practiced in the country side, mainly by people living on mountainous regions. Alternatively, numerous recipes exist for cooking lamb or goat's meat in a wood-fired oven. One such recipe was my grandfather's favourite, with the yogurt spread over the meat chucks before inserting the meat in the oven. The subtly sour yogurt crust marries extremely well with the meat.

GARDOUMAKIA AND MENOUZES

Lets start with the exotic dishes made from the intestines of the lamb. In other parts of Greece this exotic dish is known as '*mageritsa*'. However this term in not used on the island of Crete, where the animals liver (or other offal) is finely chopped and cooked in *avgolemomo* (egg and lemon sauce) and spiced with herbs (dill, fennel, and spring onions). Following a thorough cleaning and rinsing of the intestines, they are cut to approximately 2 inches long and tied to one end, then stuffed with the chopped liver and tied to the other end. These products are known as 'gardoumia'. The gardoumia are then placed in a casserole and simmered in avgolemono sauce or cooked with courgettes in red sauce.

The *menouzes* is a very small version of *kokoretsi*, with liver been one of the main ingredients. The basic ingredients for kokoretsi are: liver, lights, the guts of a lamb and oregano. A similar exotic and delicious dish is the *splenogardouma*, made from the intestines of a lamb filled with chopped spleen and cooked over live coals.

GAMOPILAFO
(Wedding Pilaf)
Serves 10

The *pilaf* served during wedding festivities in Crete is famous all over Greece. The rice is cooked in stock made from quality meat and bones. To enhance the taste of the pilaf fresh butter is also used in generous quantities. However simple this preparation may sound, it requires a skilled person with years of experience in this kind of ceremonial pilaf.

INGREDIENTS

1kg (wether) lamb

1/2 chicken

3 cups rice.

2 tablespoons fresh butter (from goat's or sheep's milk)

the juice from 1 lemon

pepper to taste

DIRECTIONS

1. Use two pots and bring the lamb and chicken to boil, respectively.

2. When all meat is done, remove it from the pots, but keep the stock. Keep the meat warm and determine the quantity of your stock (chicken and lamb). For the 3 cups of rice, you will need approximately 10–11 cups of stock.

3. Bring the stock to a boil and add 1 tablespoon of salt. Add the rice and stir well. Continue cooking until the rice has absorbed all the liquids in the pot.

4. When the rice is done, turn off the heat and remove the pot from the ring; pour in the lemon juice and stir. Heat the butter and pour it over the rice. Stir and cover the pot with a cotton towel (alternatively, place the cover askew on the pot). Let the pilaf rest for 10 minutes to absorb the remaining liquids.

5. Slice the meat to pieces and serve it in a large plate.

6. Serve the *pilaf* in standard plates and sprinkle it with pepper to taste.

SFAKIANO ASPROYACHNI
(white stew)
Serves 8-10

INGREDIENTS

4-5 cups olive oil

4-5 tablespoons red wine

1 1/2 kg lamb (from shoulder), sliced to small pieces

salt to taste

DIRECTIONS

1. Wash the meat thoroughly and let it strain. Sprinkle it with ample salt and place it in a heavy, non-stick bottom casserole. Add the olive oil, which must cover all the small pieces of meat.

2. Place the casserole, with lid on, on the oven ring and cook at high heat for 5-8 minutes. Subsequently, remove the lid and add 3/4 cups of water and continue cooking the lamb at same temperature for at least 45-50 minutes.

3. Remove the meat using a perforated spoon and serve it warm in its sauce.

STUFFED LAMB SHOULDER
Serves 6

INGREDIENTS

1 shoulder (incl. neck) of lamb

3 onions, large and finely chopped

1 kg minced meat, veal

3 cups meat stock

2 cups rice

1/2 cup olive oil

1 cup pine nuts

1 teaspoon cloves, pulverized

1 leveled teaspoon cinnamon

3 lemons, the juice of

2 tablespoons flour

dill (to taste), chopped

salt and pepper to taste

DIRECTIONS

1. In a pot sauté the onions with the minced meat for 5 minutes. Then add the stock, rice and boil for 10 minutes.

2. Add the dill, cloves, cinnamon, pine nuts, salt, pepper and cook the mixture for 5 more minutes.

3. Make a large incision (or more than one incision) in the shoulder of the lamb to tack the filling in. Sew the incision(s) with kitchen string and wrap the lamb in grease paper.

4. Baste the lamb with fresh butter, sprinkle with salt and pepper and pour half the lemon juice over the entire length of the meat. Cook in a preheated oven at 200ºC for 90 minutes. During the period of cooking, open the oven door, slide out the tray and sprinkle over the lamb the flour and lemon juice in installments.

5. When the lamb is done, curve and serve it warm.

LAMB WITH ARTICHOKE HEARTS
Serves 7–8

INGREDIENTS

1kg lamb (shoulder/leg), cubed

6-7 spring onions

1 bunch dill

1/2 cup olive oil

800gr artichoke hearts, fresh or frozen

3 lemons (the juice), plus 1 lemon cut to small slices

2 eggs

a little flour or corn flour

salt & freshly ground pepper to taste

DIRECTIONS

1. If you use fresh artichokes, remove the outer leaves until you reach beyond the tender leaves and get the hearts. Slice the artichoke hearts and remove their fuzzy centers (chokes). Place the hearts in a bowl of water with the lemon slices.

2. Rinse the meat and pat it dry, then sprinkle it with the salt and pepper. Finely chop the dill and spring onions. Heat the olive oil in a casserole to brown the meat along with the dill and onions. Pour in a little warm water and simmer for 1 hour. Then add to the meat and artichokes, a little warm water and simmer for 45–50 minutes.

3. How to make the avgolemono sauce: whisk the eggs well and gradually pour in the lemon juice. Remove a little from the stock and thicken it with a little flour or corn flour; stir and pour it in the eggs. This is your avgolemono.

4. Pour the avgolemono over the meat and sprinkle with a lot of freshly ground pepper. Mix all ingredients by shaking the casserole with your hands.

LAMB WITH DILL IN EGGS & LEMON JUICE (*AVGOLEMONO*)
Serves 7–8

INGREDIENTS

1kg lam (cubed)

1 bunch dill, finely chopped

4-5 spring onions

1/2 cup olive oil

3 eggs

1 large lemon, the juice of

DIRECTIONS

1. Rinse the meat well; sprinkle it with salt and sauté the same with onions in a casserole with olive oil. Then add half a glass of water and simmer over very low heat for 3/4 of an hour with the casserole lid on. Then add the dill, stir and let the meat boil for 15 more minutes.

2. To prepare the eggs & lemon juice (avgolemono): wire whisk the whites adding the yolks gradually, a little water, the lemon juice and stock from the meat in the casserole. When the avgolemono is ready, take the casserole off the heat and pour in the avgolemono. Don't forget to turn off heat!

CASSEROLE YOUVETSI WITH VEGETABLES AND LAMB OR *TOURLOU*

Serves 8-10

INGREDIENTS

1kg lamb (boneless leg), sliced to small pieces

2 leeks, sliced 3-4 cm long

1 cup okras

1 potato, large and cut to four pieces

1 carrot, large and chopped

1 cup green beans

1 tablespoon parsley, coarsely chopped

1 tablespoon lovage, coarsely chopped

2 courgettes, chopped

2 tomatoes, diced

1 medium-sized lemon, the juice of

3/4 cup olive oil

salt & pepper to taste

DIRECTIONS

1. Choose a large and heavy bottom casserole to sauté the meat in olive oil for 7-8 minutes, or until brown on all sides. Remove the meat using a perforated spoon and add all the vegetables in the casserole, which you have previously washed but not dried completely.

2. Then add the meat, lemon juice, salt, pepper and 1/2 cup water. Put the lid on the casserole and cook at low temperature for at least 1 hour. Do not remove the lid form the casserole until the meal is done.

3. Serve the meal hot, warm or at room temperature.

ROAST LEG OF LAMB WITH GARLIC AND POTATOES

Serves 8-10

INGREDIENTS

1 leg of lamb (approx. 1 1/2 kg)

1 kg potatoes, small

2 cloves garlic

1/2 cup olive oil

1 teaspoon oregano

1 sprig rosemary

1 teaspoon salt

1 teaspoon pepper

DIRECTIONS

1. Rinse the leg of lamb and pat it dry with kitchen paper. Using a sharp knife, make 4-5 incisions on the meat to insert a piece of garlic. Rub the leg of lamb with a little mixture made from a little salt, pepper and oregano.

2. Place the lamb in a baking dish; arrange the potatoes around it and sprinkle the entire ensemble with the olive oil, salt and pepper to taste, oregano and rosemary. Insert the dish in the oven the cook at 180°C for 60-80 minutes. Serve warm.

LAMB WITH VINE SHOOTS

Serves 8-10

INGREDIENTS

1kg lamb (shoulder/leg), cut to portions

1/2 cup olive oil

1/2 kg tender vine shoots

1/2 chicory

1 bunch dill

6-7 spring onions, coarsely chopped

1 bunch parsley, finely chopped

2 eggs

2 lemons, the juice of

salt and pepper to taste

DIRECTIONS

1. Use a large casserole to brown the meat in olive oil, then add the dill and as much water as to cover the ingredients in the casserole completely. Let them simmer.

2. Bring the vine shoots and chicory to a boil in water. When the meat is half done, transfer the shoots and chicory into the casserole with the meat, along with the dill and onions.

3. Add a little water to the casserole and let the contents boil until done. Turn off the heat and prepare the egg and lemon sauce (avgolemono): use a bowl to whisk the eggs well (using wire) and gradually add the lemon juice into the bowl. Do the same with stock from the casserole, whisking at the same time. This is your avgolemono sauce in the bowl. Slowly, pour the avgolemono into the casserole and stir continuously.

4. Serve the meal warm or at room temperature.

ROAST GOAT'S MEAT WITH SPAGHETTI
Serves 8-10

INGREDIENTS

1kg goat's meat or wether lamb cut to medium-sized slices

2 tomatoes, large and mashed

1 teaspoon tomato paste

1 onion, medium-sized and finely chopped

1 cup olive oil

salt and pepper to taste

1 packet spaghetti (penne or ditali)

a lot of grated cheese (anthotyro / ricotta) or salty gruyere

DIRECTIONS

1. Use a pan to sauté the onion in olive oil for 1-2 minutes. Add the meat to brown on all sides. Add two cups of water; cover the pan and simmer for 20-30 minutes.

2. Uncover the pan and add the salt, pepper and tomato. Continue cooking for 20-30 minutes.

3. Use a perforated spoon to remove the meat and keep it warm aside. Add as much water as may be required. Bring the water to a boil and add the spaghetti. When the spaghetti is done, top it with a lot of grated cheese and serve it with the meat.

LAMB WITH YOGURT
Serves 7-8

INGREDIENTS

1kg lamb (leg slices)

3 cups yogurt (without the skin)

1 tablespoon butter

1/2 cup olive oil

2 eggs

nutmeg, coarsely chopped

salt & pepper to taste

DIRECTIONS

1. Use a clay vessel (set lid aside) to layer in the meat. Sprinkle the meat with salt, add the olive oil and baste meat with butter. Do not add any water. The meat will cook in its own juices. Cover the clay vessel and insert it into a preheated oven to roast at 180-200ºC for an hour. Remove the cover and roast for 20 more minutes.

2. Use a bowl to wire whisk the yogurt, eggs, spices until you get a thick, homogenous mixture. Pour this mixture over the meat and continue roasting for 15-20 minutes, until you get a golden brown crust over it. No lemon juice is required if the yogurt is slightly sour in taste.

OLIVE OIL FOR

RABBIT STUFFED WITH ASSORTED CHEESE

Serves 7-8

INGREDIENTS

1 rabbit (approx. 2kg)

1/2 kg soft, Cretan myzithra or ricotta

1/3 kg Gruyere, diced small

2 tablespoons butter

3 tablespoons olive oil

oregano to taste

salt to pepper to taste

DIRECTIONS

1. Baste the rabbit with butter and sprinkle it with salt and pepper. Insert the myzithra / ricotta, the gruyere, the oregano and a little butter in the belly of the rabbit.

2. Sew the rabbit's belly using a cord; pour the olive oil over the rabbit and sprinkle it with a little more oregano and wrap it in aluminum foil. Insert the rabbit in the oven at 180oC for 1 1/2 hours. Remove the foil and brown it on the grill.

RABBIT STUFFED WITH RICE

Serves 8-10

INGREDIENTS

1 rabbit, medium size

1 kg liver (from lamb or fowls of the air), finely chopped

1 cup pine nuts

1 cup white wine, dry

1 cup rice

3/4 cup dill, finely chopped

2 onions, medium-sized and finely chopped

1/2 cup currants, brown

3/4 cups olive oil

1 lemon, the juice of

a little thyme

DIRECTIONS

1. Wash the rabbit thoroughly and remove the intestines/entrails/offal. Prepare the stuffing as follows: use a shallow pan to sauté the onions in a little olive oil until they get a little brown. Add the liver chops and stir until they absorb all liquids.

2. Pour in the wine, dill, salt & pepper to taste, a little water and let all simmer for 10 minutes. Add the rice, pine nuts, 3 cups of water and let the stuffing simmer. Five minutes before you take the pan off the heat, add the currants, stir, taste and correct with a little salt/pepper if required. Set the stuffing aside to cool down.

3. Season the interior of the rabbit and stuff it with the mixture from the pan, which you had previously set aside. Sew the rabbit's belly tight and tie the front and rear legs using a kitchen twine. Place the rabbit in a deep fireproof cookware and cover with a lid. Preheat your oven at 200ºC. Make enough sauce for three applications (see below) using the lemon juice, olive oil and thyme.

4. Season the exterior of the rabbit and pour some of the sauce over it. Insert the rabbit in a preheated oven and cook for 2 hours at medium temperature. During the cooking period, baste the rabbit with the sauce and cover the cookware with its lid to keep the rabbit moist.

5. When the rabbit is done, remove the twine, cord and the stuffing. Slice it to pieces, garnish it all around with its stuffing and pour the rest of the sauce all over. Serve warm.

RABBIT STEW

Serves 6-8

INGREDIENTS

1 rabbit, sliced to small pieces

1kg onions

2 bay leaves

a few black pepper seeds

a few red pepper seeds

1 cinnamon stick

a few cloves

1 cup red wine

DIRECTIONS

1. Use a pan to sauté the meat in olive oil on low heat for 10 minutes approximately. Turn the meat over several times to sauté uniformly.

2. Add 1 1/2 cups of water, the bay leaves, pepper seeds, cinnamon and cloves.

3. Cover the pan and simmer for 5 minutes for the spices to let their juices out.

4. Add 1 kg onions sliced; turn the heat up and let the meat come to a boil. Then add the red wine and cover the pan. Continue cooking for 3/4 of an hour with the lid on. Serve warm.

CHICKEN WITH OKRAS

Serves 6-8

INGREDIENTS

1 chicken cut to portions

1 cup olive oil

1kg okras, fresh / frozen or canned

1 large onion cut to thin slices

2 ripe tomatoes, mashed

2 large tomatoes, sliced from side to side

1 lemon, the juice of

salt, pepper & cumin to taste

DIRECTIONS

1. Clean the okras and chop their caps off. If they are too long, you can cut them in half. Rinse, drain (through a colander) and place the okras in a baking pan and sprinkle them with salt. Pour the lemon juice over them. Rinse the chicken cuts and season with salt, pepper and cumin.

2. Again drain the okras and mix them with the mashed tomato. Season them with a little more salt and pepper.

3. Place the chicken cuts in a baking pan and uniformly spread the okras over the cuts. Pour in the olive oil and add the tomato and onion slices. Cover the pan with aluminum foil and cook in a preheated oven at 180ºC for 30 minutes. Remove foil and continue cooking for 25 more minutes.

GIOUVETSI CHICKEN IN THE OVEN

Serves 8

INGREDIENTS

1 chicken cut to pieces

2 large and ripe tomatoes cut to thin rings

1 packet risoni pasta

1 medium-sized onion cut to four

2 tablespoons olive oil

1 tablespoon fresh butter

salt and pepper to taste

grated cheese

DIRECTIONS

1. Rinse the meat; cut it to large pieces and place cuts into a clay cookware that you can later cover. Pour in the olive oil; add two cups of water and spread the tomato rings over the meat. Cover the cookware with its lid and insert it in a preheated oven to cook at 200ºC for 45-50 minutes. Lower temperature to 180ºC and continue cooking for 1 more hour.

2. As soon as the meat is done, use a pot to boil the risoni and the onions in water for 5 minutes, then strain the water and stir the risoni with butter. Stir vigorously to melt the butter. Add salt & pepper to taste.

3. Uncover the clay cookware and add in the risoni around the meat. Sprinkle the meat with a little salt and pepper. Put the lid back on the clay cookware and continue cooking at 200ºC for 8 more minutes. Turn off the heat and let the meal rest in the oven for 20 minutes before you serve it with a lot of grated cheese.

STEWED CHICKEN
Serves 8-10

INGREDIENTS

1 chicken cubed for stew meat

2 onions, finely chopped

4 potatoes, medium-sized and

cut to four pieces

1 cup olive oil

3 tomatoes, grated

1 glass wine, red aromatic

salt and pepper to taste

DIRECTIONS

1. Use a pan to sauté the onions in olive oil. Add the chicken cuts and sauté them for 6-7 minutes. Add a little water and the salt to simmer for 25 minutes.

2. Next, add the potatoes, tomatoes, wine, pepper and cook until all water evaporates from the pan. Serve warm.

OVEN CHICKEN WITH POTATOES AND OREGANO
Serves 8-10

INGREDIENTS

1 chicken cut in half

2kg potatoes, medium-sized &

cut to four

2 lemons, the juice of

1/2 cup olive oil

1 teaspoon oregano

salt and pepper to taste

DIRECTIONS

1. Rinse the chicken halves well under tap water, pat them dry and place them in a roasting pan.

2. Pour half of the lemon juice over and season them with oregano, salt and pepper. Arrange the potatoes around the chicken halves and pour the remaining lemon juice over the potatoes. Also, season the potatoes with oregano, salt and pepper. Use your hands to mix them a little.

3. Pour olive oil over the chicken and the potatoes and place the roasting pan in a preheated oven to cook at 180-200ºC for 1 1/2 approximately. If all the juice evaporates, add a little water during the cooking period.

VEAL STEW
Serves 7-8

INGREDIENTS

1kg veal (shoulder or neck parts)

1kg onions, small

1 cup olive oil

3/4 cup tomato paste

1 teaspoon cloves

1 cinnamon stick

4 bay leaves

4 basil leaves

sugar, salt, pepper: to taste

DIRECTIONS

1. Slice meat to 1 1/2 inch cubes. Peel, rinse and place the onions in water for 30 minutes. Add two onions whole and the meat cubes in a casserole to brown a little on all sides.

2. Add a little water to casserole and simmer for 35 minutes. Add the cinnamon, bay leaves, cloves, salt, pepper, the rest of the onions whole, tomato paste (dissolved in water), basil leaves and sugar. Cook for 40 more minutes at 200ºC. Add a little water if required.

YOUVARLAKIA
(meat & rice balls in soup)
Serves 7-8

NGREDIENTS

1kg minced meat (veal)

1/2 lt stock made from boiled calf bones

2 tablespoons parsley, finely chopped

1 onion, large & finely chopped

1/2 teaspoon pepper

1 teaspoon cumin, leveled

3 tablespoons rice

2 eggs

the juice from 2 lemons

DIRECTIONS

1. Use a bowl to mix the minced meat with the onion, parsley, rice, pepper and cumin. Make round balls out of the mixture, the size of a walnut. Mix the stock with 1/5 lt of water in a pot and let come to a boil; then add the meat balls and cook for 40 minutes at 180ºC. When done, remove the pot from heat.

2. In the meantime prepare the eggs and lemon (*avgolemono*) sauce: whisk the eggs in a deep bowl and add the lemon juice and gradually an equal amount or more of stock from the pot, whisking at the same time. When done, pour the avgolemono sauce into the pot in small installments stirring at the same time.

3. Serve the youvarlakia hot or warm.

CHICKPEAS WITH VEAL or BEEF

Serves 8-10

INGREDIENTS

1 cup olive oil plus 2
tablespoons of the same
2 cups chickpeas soaked in
water for 12 hours
.1 kg veal or beef (cubed)
1 onion, large and grated
1 tomato, ripe and cut
to small cubes
1/2 teaspoon tomato paste
1/2 teaspoon cumin
1 teaspoon lemon juice
1/2 teaspoon grated lemon rind
salt and pepper to taste

DIRECTIONS

1. Boil the chickpeas in a lot of water for 15 minutes approximately, then strain.
2. Use a pan to sauté the onion in olive oil for 3-4 minutes until lightly brown. Add the meat, stir and brown it on all sides. Add 2 cups of water and cover the pan to cook for 35-49 minutes.
3. Test meat with a fork to see if it is done, in which case you add the chickpeas, tomato and the tomato paste (previously dissolved in 1/2 cup of water). Stir the ingredients in the pan for 3-4 minutes and season with the salt and pepper in installments while stirring. Add 7-8 cups of water and cook for 30-35 more minutes.
4. Remove the cover and lower heat. Add the cumin, the lemon juice and grated lemon rind. Stir the ingredients and let the meal cook for 3-4 more minutes without covering the pan.
5. Serve the meal warm or in room temperature and sprinkle with a lot of pepper.

MEATBALLS

Serves 8-10

INGREDIENTS

1/2 kg minced meat (veal)
1/2 kg minced meat (pork)
2 onions, large and grated
1 tomato, finely grated
1/2 loaf of bread, only the
breadcrumbs
3 tablespoons milk
1 egg
1 teaspoon mint
1 teaspoon cumin, leveled
1 cup flour, hard
salt and pepper to taste
1 1/2 cups olive oil for frying

DIRECTIONS

1. Mix all ingredients in a large bowl, preferably by hand. Make sure the mixture is not very thick − rather a little thin.
2. Refrigerate the mixture for 20 minutes. Subsequently, knead all ingredients to walnut size balls. Roll balls on a thin layer of flour and fry them in hot olive oil.

Fish and the Cretan cuisine

Ancient sources provide us with significant information concerning marine species and fish-food recipes. Aristotle, for example, wrote a treatise on fish ("On Fish"). Other observations and treatises were by Archippus (an Athenian epicurean), Dorion ("On Fish"), Numenius the philosopher ("On Fishing"), Euthydemus ("On Salt-fish"), Antiphanes ("How-to-Fish" Essay), Oppianus (Fish and Fishing methods), a.o

The Cretan Sea offered a wide variety of fish in the old days, while the small-bodied ancient Cretans (the "*Keftiu*") were expert fishermen and keen fishmongers. They used small and flexible boats to furrow the Cretan and Libyan Seas. The main tools of their trade were hooks made from copper or bones, string from animal hairs or even vegetable fiber and various plummets (stone or lead). To trap fish, they used weir baskets, and nets of various sizes and complexity. The nets were rigged with hooks, floats and plummets. Also, harpoons were used to catch larger fish, and scoop nets for ease of pulling smaller fish on boats. The ancients fished mainly at dawn and nightfall. Night fishing required a source of light – torches lit and fixed on boats.

Fishing was an invaluable source of income for many coastal towns of Crete. Actually, the economy of many ancient Cretan towns along the coasts depended exclusively on fishing. Evidence to this is provided by numerous finds in the form of murals, coins and seals depicting marine species (fish, mollusks and clams).

The golden Scarus (parrot fish), a piece of jewellery worn around the neck of women in the Minoan period, provides testimony to the unbroken link between the marine fauna of Crete in the remote past and that of the present.

markets abound with fish". This chapter presented a survey of 765 Cretan families in terms of their nutritional habits in 1948."

NUTRITIONAL VALUE

Fish is of high nutritional value, as it is rich in albumen, vitamins and calcium. This explains why fish is highly recommended for children and the aged. Besides, the fatty substances it includes are quite beneficial to us: it sustains a balanced health, without adding unnecessary calories. It nourishes the skin and keeps the joints in perfect working condition.

In addition, fish reduces cholesterol and triglycerides; helps the development of the brain and enhances visual acuity. Furthermore, fish reduces incidents of heart attack, cancer growths and atherosclerosis.

Nutrition specialists focus their attention all the more on the "blue fatty substances" of such fish as sardines,

DAYS OF FASTING AND FISH-EATING

The 25th of March is one of the most important fish-eating days, as it coincided with the period of meat abstinence before Easter (Lent). Another day is Palm Sunday. More meat- fasting days are in mid-August, and before the 6th of August (the Transfiguration of Our Lord). To sustain remembrance of fasting and fish-eating days, the Cretans coined a number of popular sayings. For the Virgin Mary feast, for example, they would say: "The names Mary and John stand for fish in the pan!" For the Palm Sunday and the 15-day period of fasting that follows, Cretans prepared fish, preferably chub mackerel. "Tomorrow begins the Palm Feast, days for fish and chub mackerel, while Sunday is the day for a fat lamb". Fish-eating is allowed during the fasting period prior to Christmas, until December 17.

In a case study of Crete by Leland Allbaugh (with editorial assistance from George Soule) – CRETE: A Case Study of an Underdeveloped Area, Princeton, New Jersey Princeton University Press, 1953 – the author notes the following in Chapter 6, Food and Nutrition: "During the period of research, the cod, particularly the salted, dry type, was very much consumed. Other salted fish consumed were the sea rover, sardines, and cuttlefish. The average consumption of fresh fish was approximately 75gr per capita per week, which was the same both for urban centres and the hinterland. However, the amount of fresh fish consumed in urban centres was three times more than the amount consumed in the hinterland. Among the fresh fish consumed were the picarel (bulg), red mullet, and octopus. The annual consumption of fresh fish during the period of the case study was the highest of the year. Autumn is one of the two seasons when the fish

scads (horse mackerel), anchovies. These fats have a unique function: they reduce triglyceride and cholesterol levels, thus mitigating the frequency of heart diseases; they also protect the muscular system and women from osteoporosis, while they promote the good function of the nervous system

SEA WEEDS

In the coastal area of Kissamos, prefecture of Hania, the local population is in the habit of consuming large quantities from a particular species of seaweed, the "*Rhodymenia*", or Dulse. This is a coarse edible red seaweed that takes purchase on rocky shores. It has a crunchy texture and can be used raw in salads, usually sprinkled with a lot of olive oil and a little vinegar. As is

the case with most seaweeds, the *Rhodymenia* is rich in mineral salts and iodine. It is collected from shallow reefs and peddled by traveling fishermen. The dark brown dulse of *Kissamos* is referred to as Sea Lettuce by the local population. It is usually cooked with other seafood, mainly shell fish mixed with potatoes.

THE *SCARUS* (PARROT FISH) OF THE CRETAN SEA

This species emerged 4,000 centuries ago, in the turquoise waters of the big "Mother" in gestation then of thousands of other marine species. The parrot fish inspired Minoan gold- and silver-smiths; enriched the menu of the ancient Greeks and is still at the top of the fish list of modern gourmets. Since this fish species is so famous, the chapter devoted to fish will not fail to start with parrot fish recipes. Actually, the ancient Greeks knew this fish species very well −in the

Encyclopaedia of the Instituto Geografico de Agostini this fish is referred to as *Euscarus Cretensis*. Today parrot fish abound in the rocky shores of Crete. Its teeth are configured somewhat like a parrot's beak, to facilitate their crunching of coral and marine flora. Actually, it is the only fish that ruminates (chews the cuds). Aristotle mentions this fish in his treatise "On Fish".

COOKING

The parrot fish is the only fish of its size that does not require any cleaning (removal of scales, stomach cavity, etc.) as long as it has had nothing to eat before it was caught. How would you know that? Unless you catch parrot fish yourselves in the early morning hours, you will never know. In the western prefectures of Crete, parrot fish is either stewed or cooked in casserole or in the oven with okras.

Also, parrot fish makes an excellent meal on charcoal, and marries well with tomato sauce, which is prepared separately. The best season to purchase parrot fish is the summer, when it abounds in the fish markets of Crete.

PARROT FISH STEW
Serves 6-8

INGREDIENTS

1 1/2 kg fresh parrot fish

1 cup olive oil

2 large onions, finely chopped

2 tomatoes, grated

1 cup wine

1 tablespoon parsley, finely chopped

1 tablespoon dill, finely chopped

salt and pepper to taste

DIRECTIONS

1. Slice the fish to fairly large cuts and season them with salt and pepper. Use a large pot to sauté the onion in olive oil for 5-6 minutes, or until golden brown.

2. Add the wine, tomato, parsley, dill, salt & pepper to taste and simmer for 15 minutes.

3. Add the fish cuts; cover the pot and continue cooking for 15 more minutes. Serve the meal warm or at room temperature.

ANCHOVIES OR SARDINES IN OREGANO
Serves 6

INGREDIENTS

1 1/2 kg sardines or anchovies

1 cup olive oil

5-6 cloves garlic, finely chopped

1-2 lemons, the juice

oregano

salt and pepper to taste

DIRECTIONS

1. Clean the fish: remove scales, stomach cavity and cut off the heads.

2. Arrange the fish in a shallow baking dish; pour in the olive oil; sprinkle with the salt & pepper, oregano, garlic, lemon juice and a little water.

3. Insert the dish in a medium heat oven and bake for 45 minutes. Serve the fish warm or at room temperature.

FISH WITH RAW TOMATO SAUCE

Serves 6

INGREDIENTS

1 kg fish in cuts (sea bream or croakers or grouper)

2 ripe tomatoes

1 large onion, finely chopped

1 lemon, the juice

1/2 cup olive oil

oregano

salt and pepper to taste

DIRECTIONS

1. Wash, clean, cut and season the fish. Place the cuts on the oven grate or on charcoal. Bake the cuts for 30 minutes at 180ºC (if in the oven). If you cook the cuts on charcoal, make sure the grate is placed at the higher rung, initially, then as the coals die down and the fish is not yet done, lower the grate.

2. Put the lemon juice, olive oil, tomatoes, onion and a tablespoon of water into a blender bowl and run it at high speed to mix all the ingredients well. Place the fish in a large plate and pour the sauce over. Serve immediately.

GROUPER WITH LEEKS AND FENNEL

Serves 6

INGREDIENTS

600gr white grouper

400gr leeks, cleaned and chopped

400gr fennel

1/4 cup olive oil

1 medium-sized tomato, finely chopped

1 medium-sized onion, chopped

1 small lemon, the juice

salt and pepper to taste

DIRECTIONS

1. Use a pan to sauté the onion in the olive oil and add the leeks and fennel to soften. Then add the tomato, salt & pepper. When the juices in the pan have been absorbed, add the ingredients of the pan into a baking dish.

2. Place the fish (previously cut to slices) in the dish and into the oven and bake at 180oC for 20 minutes. Serve warm.

FISH *PLAKI* (OVEN STEW)

Serves 6

INGREDIENTS

2kg fish (sea bream or grouper)

4-5 tomatoes, mashed

3-4 onions, finely chopped

1 bunch parsley

1 cup olive oil

1 clove garlic, mashed

1 teaspoon oregano

salt and pepper to taste

DIRECTIONS

1. Use a large baking dish to add the olive oil, tomato, onions, oregano and parsley. This will make your sauce.

2. Insert the baking dish into the oven and cook at 150ºC for 30 minutes, until the sauce forms. When the sauce is ready, place the fish into a baking dish and spoon it over with a lot of sauce. Add a little more olive oil, garlic, salt, pepper and insert the dish into the oven again to bake at 200ºC for 40 minutes. Serve the fish warm in its sauce.

FISH WITH OKRAS

Serves 6

INGREDIENTS

1kg fresh okras

1kg fish (sea bream or grouper)

1 medium-sized ripe tomato, finely chopped

1/2 tablespoon tomato paste

1 small clove garlic, finely chopped

1 large onion, finely chopped

1 cup olive oil

2 lemons, the juice

1 shot cumin

salt & pepper

DIRECTIONS

1. Clean the okras and remove their hard tops. Slice them in half, if quite large. Wash the okras and let them drain well. Sprinkle them with salt and pour half the lemon juice over them. Transfer the okras into a large baking tray to rest for an hour and drain their juices. Then, wash the okras well under tap water and transfer them into a large bowl. If you purchase frozen okras, skip the above procedure.

2. With the okras in the bowl, add the tomato, tomato paste dissolved in the other half of the lemon juice, the garlic, onion, salt, pepper, cumin and olive oil. Stir the ingredients well.

3. Use a large baking tray to place the fish. Pour the okras in the perimeter of the fish. Add one cup of water and cover the tray using foil and insert the tray into the oven. Bake at 180ºC for 1 hour and 20 minutes. During the last 20 minutes remove the foil and let the meal brown. Serve warm or at room temperature.

SAVORE FISH ON LEMON LEAVES
Serves 6

INGREDIENTS

1kg fish (snapper, mackerel, red mallet)

1 cup flour

1 1/2 glasses olive oil

1 glass vinegar (from red wine)

2 sprigs rosemary

6 lemon leaves

salt to taste

DIRECTIONS

1. Clean, wash and season the fish.

2. In the meanwhile heat the olive oil in a frying pan. Dredge fish on flour; pat them to remove loose flour and fry them in the hot olive oil until golden brown on both sides. Remove fish from the heat and transfer them on a plate lined with the clean lemon leaves.

3. Add the rosemary sprigs and the vinegar in the hot olive oil to make the sauce. Let the ingredients in the frying pan simmer for 5 minutes.

4. Pour the sauce from the pan over the fish in the plate and serve them warm or at room temperature.

Do not remove the rosemary sprigs or the lemon leaves from the plate.

SARDINE SALAD
(snack)
Serves 6-8

INGREDIENTS

3 dry-salted sardines (remove spine)

14 blanched almonds

3 slices white bread

3/4 olive oil

3-4 tablespoons strong vinegar

1 tablespoon parsley

salt, pepper

DIRECTIONS

1. Place the sardines, almonds, half the parsley, bread (soaked in water and drained well) in a blender bowl. Run the blender to mix all of the above.

2. Add the pepper, little salt and alternate between small amounts of vinegar and olive oil while the blender is running. When you have exhausted the vinegar and oil, you will have a smooth paste. Transfer the paste into a dish and sprinkle it with the remaining parsley (chopped). This is your salad. Serve it with fresh bread slices and fried fish.

FISH SOUP

Serves 8

INGREDIENTS

2kg fish (cod, grouper, bream gournard)

2 medium-sized tomatoes, sliced to 4 pieces

1/2 kg courgettes

1/2 kg carrots, sliced

1/2 cup olive oil

1 bunch parsley, coarsely chopped

1 bunch celery, coarsely chopped

2 large potatoes, cut to 4 pcs each.

2 large onions, coarsely chopped

1/2 cup rice

2 lemons, the juice

salt

pepper, freshly ground

DIRECTIONS

1. Use a large pot and fill it half with water. Add 1/2 cup olive oil and a little salt. Also, add the celery, parsley, carrots, onions, tomatoes and let them boil to 20 minutes.

2. Score the courgettes lengthwise and add them, along with the potatoes, into the pot. Then add the fish, cut to 2-3 slices if large.

3. Let all boil for 30 min. approximately. Then transfer all (fish, potatoes, courgettes and carrots) into a large dish using a perforated spoon. Keep the vegetable stock.

4. Spoon out a few carrots, courgettes, potatoes and blend them to a pulp and add pulp to the stock.

5. Bring the stock to the boil and add the rice. Add water if necessary. Continue boiling for 20 minutes. Before you turn off heat, add the lemon juice.

SHORE DINNER
(Eastern Crete speciality)
Serves 6-8

INGREDIENTS

2 kg fish (gournard, grouper, bream)
5 large potatoes, cubed
3 large onions, chopped
1 cup olive oil
2 lemons, the juice
salt

DIRECTIONS

1. Clean, wash and season the fish with salt. Cut them to slices and set them aside.

2. Use a pot to sauté the onions in the olive oil. Add the potatoes; stir and simmer for 10 minutes.

3. Place the fish on top of the potatoes and add 10 cups water. The water should barely top the fish. Cook the shore dinner over high heat for 18-20 minutes, with pot uncovered. When the soup is ready, add the lemon juice, raise and shake the pot a little. Turn off heat and let the pot with the soup rest on the hot ring for 10-15 minutes. Serve immediately after then.

Fish of the "mountain"

This is salt cod. It was first introduced to Crete during the 15th century, which explains bulk imports of cod from France to Greece in early 16th century.

The Cretans became avid consumers of this dry, salted fish for reasons that are no less different from those applying to millions of people in the Mediterranean basin.

Salt cod is cheap and can be preserved for months, not requiring refrigeration. Consequently, it could reach the mountainous villages of Crete, where it was soaked in water and cooked into a delicious meal for the families to enjoy!

In some islands, including Crete, where the soil and the terrain mobilized the entire family to farming activities, given also that the yield of the sea was poor in fish, salt cod was the fish of choice both in urban centers and the hinterland. The history of imported salt cod to Crete is a long one. For example, from the records of the Chamber of Marseilles we now know that the imports of this fish to Crete in 1768 and 1776 amounted to 25,792 lb and 49,900 lb respectively.

The Portuguese may boast of 1,000 ways of cooking salt cod, but in Tylissos of Crete the inhabitants are not only avid consumers of salt cod, but also very imaginative in making scores of dishes with this fish.

COD WITH CELERY
Serves 6-8

INGREDIENTS

1 kg salt cod

1 1/3 cups olive oil

2 ripe tomatoes, finely chopped

1 kg celery, cut to medium sizes

2 large onions, finely chopped

salt and pepper

DIRECTIONS

1. Remove (scrape) the salt off the cod and slice the fish to pieces. Put the cod pieces in water for 8-9 hours. In the while, change the water a few times.

2. Clean, wash and cut the celery, then drain it. Use a pot to sauté the celery and onion in olive oil for 7-9 minutes.

3. Use another pot to put the celery, onion and cod pieces in alternating layers.

4. Finally, add the tomato, a little more olive oil, the pepper and a cup of water. Cover the pot and cook for 50-55 minutes on moderate heat. Serve warm.

SALT COD WITH GARLIC SAUCE

Serves 6-8

INGREDIENTS

1 kg salt cod

3 cups olive oil for frying

1 teaspoon baking powder

1 cup olive oil

Garlic sauce:

6 cloves garlic

3 potatoes, boiled

3/4 cup olive oil

1 tablespoon vinegar, strong

DIRECTIONS

1. Slice the salt cod to small pieces and put them into fresh water for 10-12 hours. In the while change the water 5-6 times.

2. Rinse the pieces and remove the large bones. Use a bowl to whisk the flour and baking powder in the water to a thick pulp.

3. Dip the cod pieces into the pulp and fry them in a lot of olive oil until golden brown on both sides. Serve the cod with garlic sauce, which you prepare as follows: peal and crush the garlic in a mortar. Toss the potatoes in a blender and run it to mash them. Gradually add into the bowl the garlic, olive oil and vinegar. Run the blender to get a paste of fine texture.

OCTOPUS WITH PASTA

Serves 6

INGREDIENTS

1 kg octopus

1 packet pasta (short tube)

1 cup olive oil

1 large onion, finely chopped

3 tomatoes, grated

1/2 cup red wine

little salt

pepper

DIRECTIONS

1. Clean and run the octopus under tap water (see previous recipe). Cut it to small pieces, sauté them and the onion in a pot for 7–9 minutes.

2. Pour the wine over the octopus and let it boil for 10 minutes approximately. Then add the tomato; cover the pot and simmer for 40–45 minutes. If necessary, add a little water.

3. When the octopus is done, add 6–7 cups of water and bring it to the boil. Add the pasta, stir and continue cooking for 10–15 minutes, stirring occasionally so that the pasta does not stick to the pot. Serve warm and sprinkle with freshly grated cheese.

OCTOPUS IN A JAR

(Stored in 2 large jars)

INGREDIENTS

1 large octopus (2–3 kg)

3 cups extra virgin olive oil

2 glasses vinegar, strong from red wine

salt

DIRECTIONS

1. If the octopus is fresh, beat and rub it on a rough surface for 20–30 minutes. Alternatively, store it in the freezer for 8 hours to "soften".

2. When you are ready to cook it, first wash it under tap water and remove the beak and eyes. Then place the entire octopus into a large pot and simmer it over low heat without adding any water, just sprinkle it with a little salt.

3. Remove the octopus from the pot and chop it thinly. Place the thin slices into a frying pan with hot olive oil to brown on both sides.

4. When done, remove the octopus pieces from the pan; let them cool down and place them in glass jars topping them with virgin olive oil and a little vinegar.

OCTOPUS IN THE OVEN (snack)
Serves 8

INGREDIENTS

1 kg octopus

1 cup olive oil

1 tablespoon oregano

2 tablespoons vinegar

1/2 cup wine

salt and pepper

DIRECTIONS

1. Clean and wash the octopus (as in previous recipes) and cut it to eight (8) pieces. Boil the pieces in salted water and the vinegar for 10 minutes. Mix the olive oil, oregano and wine in a bowl to marinade the octopus pieces for 30 minutes.

2. Place the octopus pieces on the grate of your oven and grill it on both sides at 200ºC for 15 minutes.

3. Remove the octopus pieces from the oven, pour the marinade over them and sprinkle with a few drops of vinegar.

OCTOPUS BALLS
Serves 10

INGREDIENTS

1kg octopus, fresh or frozen

2 cups breadcrumbs, white

1 cup red wine

2 cups vinegar

2 large onions, finely chopped

1 tablespoon oregano

little salt

2 cups flour, for frying

freshly ground pepper

olive oil for frying

DIRECTIONS

1. Clean octopus with a small sharp knife. Cut off head, or slit open, and remove gut, ink sack. Pick up body, push beak up with index finger; remove and discard. Clean octopus well under running water; pat dry with paper towel. Place octopus in freezer for 3–4 days to "soften", particularly if octopus is fresh.

2. When you are ready to make balls out of the octopus, remove it from the freezer and let it thaw before you insert it whole into the minced–meat machine. Alternatively, you could cut it into very small pieces, but this requires skill and extra time.

3. Place the minced or finely cut octopus into a colander and let it drain.

4. Soak the breadcrumbs in the mixture of wine and vinegar. Strain the crumbs dry with your hands and add them to the octopus, along with the onion, oregano, salt and pepper. If your mixture is thin, add a tablespoon of flour. Pick up a little from the mixture and make a ball the size of a walnut. Repeat until you have exhausted the mixture. Fry the octopus balls in hot olive oil.

5. When the balls are ready, remove them from the frying pan using a perforated spatula and place them on a large dish lined with kitchen paper. Serve them warm or at room temperature.

OCTOPUS IN WINE
(snack)
Serves 8-10

INGREDIENTS

1 kg octopus

1/2 water glass olive oil

1 cup red wine

salt, pepper

DIRECTIONS

1. Clean and wash the octopus very well and slice it to small pieces. If the octopus is fresh, you need to beat, pound and rub it on a rough surface from 20-30 minutes to soften it. Alternatively, you may put it in a freezer for 24 hours.

2. Put the octopus pieces in a shallow, non-stick frying pan to simmer them in their juices at 100ºC for 10 minutes.

3. When the octopus has absorbed all of its juice, add two glasses of water and the olive oil.

4. While cooking, test tenderness using a fork. Having established that the octopus is almost done, gradually add the wine and stir at the same time, to make the sauce. Serve warm.

STUFFED CALAMARI (SQUID)

Serves 6

INGREDIENTS

1kg medium-sized calamari

1 cup olive oil

1 cup rice

1 ripe tomato, finely chopped

2 large onions, finely chopped

1 clove garlic, mashed

2 tablespoons parsley, finely chopped

1/2 lemon, the juice

salt, pepper

DIRECTIONS

1. Clean the calamari and wash it thoroughly under tap water. Cut off the heads and remove the eyes; set the heads aside. Finely chop the tentacles and the heads.

2. To make the filling: use a pot to sauté the finely chopped onion and garlic in half the quantity of olive oil for 2-3 minutes. Add in the copped heads and tentacles. Season with salt & pepper; pour one half of the lemon juice over, one half of the tomatoes, the entire quantity of chopped parsley and a cup of water.

3. Let all simmer for 15 min. approximately. Add 2 cups of water and the rice. Stir well. Simmer with the pot uncovered until all juices have been absorbed. Let the filling cool down.

4. Use a spoon to stuff the cuttlefish − not entirely. Secure the openings using a toothpick. Arrange the stuffed cuttlefish in a pyrex dish. Pour the rest of the olive oil over them, the rest of the lemon juice and 1/2 cup of water. Cover the pyrex dish with aluminum foil and insert it in a preheated oven to bake for 40-45 minutes. During the last 10 minutes remove the foil and let the calamari brown on top.

5. Serve warm or at room temperature and pour the sauce over.

CUTTLEFISH IN INK

Serves 8-10

INGREDIENTS

1kg fresh cuttlefish, small

1 1/2 cups olive oil

1 large onion, grated

4 tablespoons white wine

salt

DIRECTIONS

1. Clean the cuttlefish, by removing the cuttlebone, guts and ink (save 3-4 ink sacks). Run the cuttlefish under tap water and slice them to small pieces, if the cuttlefish are too large.

2. Heat the olive oil in a pot to sauté the onion, until it gets translucent. Add in the cuttlefish pieces and brown them on all sides, then pour in the wine. Add 2 cups of water, stir and cover the pot to simmer for 40-45 minutes.

3. Uncover the pot, add in the ink and salt, stir in vigorously using a fork and continue cooking for 20-25 minutes, with the pot uncovered, until the cuttlefish is done.

SHRIMPS IN OIL & LEMON SAUCE

Serves 8

INGREDIENTS

1kg shrimps (fresh or frozen)

1 cup water

1 tablespoon salt

Oil & Lemon sauce:

4-5 tablespoons virgin olive oil

1 small lemon, the juice

salt & pepper

DIRECTIONS

1. Boil the shrimps in salted water for 10 minutes, with the cooking vessel covered.

2. Drain and let shrimps cool down. Remove shells and heads and place shrimps' meat in a bowl.

3. The sauce: pick a jar that you can seal airtight. Put all sauce ingredients in the jar; seal and shake it well to get a "creamy" liquid. Pour this liquid (your sauce) over the shrimps and serve immediately.

Sea Urchins

Well, the taste of urchins (the roe) is associated with extreme feelings on both sides of the taste spectrum. You either find them delicious or revolting.

Urchins abound in some parts of Greece. You can find them along the coasts of Crete, Peloponnese and the Cyclades. Urchins (the roe) are delicacies served in oil and lemon sauce in restaurants and taverns. You can find urchin roe salad in the fish taverns of Hania, Heraklion, Cefalonia, isle of Ikaria, Halkidiki peninsula and Kavala.

HOW TO "CLEAN" URCHINS

• "Fish" them out from the sea and place them under a shady place to keep them alive for as long as it takes before you "clean" them.

• To extract the roe you must pry them open, in which case you will need a fork or a special scissors or cutter. However, a fork will do, but you will also need one glove (work or industrial type) to hold the urchin, a little spoon, a glass jar or a plastic bowl.

• Put on the glove and place one urchin in your gloved palm. Pick a fork (face up) and insert the point of its left-end tine into the urchin's mouth (center). Make sure that the point of the second tine does not pierce through the urchin. Push the point a little deeper into the urchin so that the urchin's pierced-through shell is between the first and the second tine of the fork. In doing so, give the fork a clockwise turn (in relation to one of the urchin's meridian) thus cracking the shell caught between the two tines. A little counter-clockwise movement will allow you to insert the left tine deeper into the shell. Repeat the clockwise cutting motion until you have reached the urchin's "equator". If cut pieces of shell accumulate at the root of the fork, remove them by hand. Now, you can continue cutting sideways (along its equator) to come to a complete circle and thus remove the top (cap). Remember, the cutting of the shell takes place only when the shell is between the first two tines. This operation will expose the interior of the urchin. Good luck!

• Use the tail end of the little spoon to remove the "orange" roe (usually laid in a star like fashion) and place it in the jar or bowl. Remove grit from the roe, if any. Repeat the cutting and harvesting of roe operation until you have exhausted all urchins "fished". 20-30 urchins will suffice for a little urchin salad.

• Whole urchins can be preserved in the fridge for 1-2 days and cleaned urchins for 3-4 days. However, we recommend that you consume them immediately.

URCHIN ROE SALAD

Serves 6

INGREDIENTS

25-35 urchins

1 1/2 tablespoon extra virgin olive oil

1 tablespoon lemon juice, fresh

DIRECTIONS

1. Use a knife or special scissors to cut down (meridian) on the urchin through its mouth (center) and then along its equator, to remove the top (cap). This will expose the interior of the urchin. You may need to wear protective hand gear for this operation. Detailed instructions are given above.

2. Use a little spoon to remove the "orange" roe (usually laid in a star like fashion) and place it in a deep dish or bowl. Remove grit, if any.

3. When you have exhausted all urchins. Add the olive oil and lemon juice in the bowl or dish. Stir and serve immediately. Best consumed with white bread.

CUTTLEFISH WITH FENNEL AND SPINACH

Serves 6

INGREDIENTS

1 kg cuttlefish

1 cup fennel

2 cups chopped spinach

2 spring onions

1 small onion, finely sliced

1 medium size tomato, cubed

the juice from 1 large lemon

1 cup olive oil

salt

pepper

DIRECTIONS

1. Clean and rinse the cuttlefish well.

2. Pick a large heavy-bottom pot and heat the olive oil. Stir-fry the onion for 1-2 minutes then add the cuttlefish to brown on both sides. Add 3 cups of water, cover pot with lid and simmer for at least 40-45 minutes.

3. Add the spinach, fennel, spring onions, tomato, salt, pepper and, if required, a little water. Cove pot with lid and continue cooking at low temperature unit the greens are soft.

4. Pour the lemon juice and stir well. Let the meal rest for 10-15 minutes before you serve.

Legumes (Pulses)

In terms of dietary habits, a significant difference between the Cretans and other Europeans was that the former consumed considerably larger quantities of legumes. Until the late 1960's vegetables and legumes represented the food for the poor, and the staple for Cretans living in the hinterland of the island. Broad beans (*kyami*) are the most common legumes on Crete. They are made stew, after they are shelled and mashed. Other common legumes are: the lupins (*thérmi*), chickpeas (*erévinthi*), lentils, green beans and split peas puree (*fava*) (*étnos*). A most interesting practice was the mixing of legumes with other garden or field produce: for example, the mixing of legumes with wild or cultivated herbs (i.e. spinach, fennel, onion, etc.). One day-old cooked legumes can be fried just like meat-balls (*favokeftédes*) or combined with cereals (rice or frumenty).

OLIVE OIL AND LEGUMES

There is a saying which describes how fast legumes (lentils, broad beans, etc.) absorb the olive oil: "There goes the olive oil, the lentils guzzled it all ....". This popular saying describes in a most 'picturesque' manner the delectable consummation of legumes and olive oil, the marrying of both into a delicious and nutritious meal.

NUTRITIONAL VALUE

Legumes (grains) form the base of the Food Guide Pyramid and have a high nutritional value as they are rich in proteins, unsaturated fat and complex hydrocarbons. They are an excellent source of fibre, in contrast to other protein sources (meat, fish, eggs, cheeses) with no fibre content. In addition, legumes are a very good source for calcium, iron, magnesium and thiamine.

HOW TO COOK LEGUMES

A word of caution here, in view of the popular misconception that adding soda in legumes makes them more tender and shortens the cooking time. The fact is that soda eliminates precious vitamins of the B complex. Also, do not shell legumes (excepting perhaps in some recipes involving broad beans). The shells of grains contain precious elements. To make shells tender, you could add the salt in the end of the boiling period. Most importantly, however, we strongly recommend the soaking of legumes and other grains in water overnight. This reduces the cooking period.

CHICKPEAS WITH MEAT BALLS

Serves 8

INGREDIENTS

2 cups of chick-peas (boiled)

for the meat balls
1/2 kg minced meat (veal)
1/2 kg minced meat (pork)
1 slice of bread
1 tablespoon toasted slice of
bread (crumbled)
2 medium-sized onions,
mashed
2 tablespoons vinegar
1 teaspoon salt
1 teaspoon pepper
1 teaspoon cumin
1/2 teaspoon oregano

for the sauce:
1/2 cup olive oil
2 ripe tomatoes, mashed
1 medium-sized onion, grated
salt and pepper to taste

DIRECTIONS

1. Use a large bowl to mix the minced meat with the bread (which you have previously soaked in water and drained), the crumbled toast, the onions, vinegar, salt, pepper, cumin and oregano. Knead the mixture with your hands to mix all ingredients well. Then set the mixture aside.

2. Make the sauce: sauté the onion in olive oil, or until the onions lightly brown, then add the tomatoes, salt & pepper, and 1/2 cup water.

3. Pick a handful from the mixture in item 1 above and make a ball the size of medium walnut. Repeat the ball making process until you have exhausted the mixture. These are your meat balls.

4. Bring the sauce to a boil and add the meat balls, chickpeas and let the meal simmer for 15 minutes

BROAD BEANS STEW

Serves 8

INGREDIENTS

2 cups broad beans (soaked for 8 hours)

1 1/2 cups olive oil

3 large onions, coarsely chopped

1 large and ripe tomato, chopped

1 teaspoon tomato paste

2 cloves garlic, finely chopped

1 tablespoon parsley

2 bay leaves

1 teaspoon cumin

1 teaspoon salt

1 teaspoon sugar

1 teaspoon pepper

2 tablespoons vinegar

DIRECTIONS

1. Boil the broad beans in a pot with a lot of water for 30 minutes, then strain.

2. Pour the olive oil in a heavy-bottom casserole to sauté the onion and garlic for 4-5 minutes, or until lightly brown. Add the broad beans (minus 6-10 pieces), stir and add the tomatoes, the tomato paste (dissolved in a cup of water), all the spices, parsley, sugar, salt, pepper and a cup of water. Cover the casserole and simmer for 20 minutes.

3. Shell the 6-10 pieces of broad beans you have kept aside and add them and the vinegar to the casserole. Stir, raise the heat and cook for 10 more minutes without the lid on the casserole. Serve the stew warm or at room temperature.

LIMA BEANS WITH *APAKI* (SMOKED PORK)

Serves 8

INGREDIENTS

1 kg lima beans

1/2 kg *apaki*, cubed

1/2 cup olive oil

2 fresh tomatoes, grated

1 large onion, finely chopped

1 clove garlic, finely chopped

1 bay leaf

salt, pepper and oregano to taste

DIRECTIONS

1. Soak the lima beans in fresh water for 8-10 hours to swell.

2. Strain and boil the beans in a lot of salted water for 10 minutes.

3. Strain and dispose of the salted water. Bring the beans to a boil in 1/2 lt. of fresh water, along with all the other ingredients, excepting the *apaki* (smoked pork).

4. Transfer the contents of the pot, and the *apaki*, into a baking pan. Insert the pan into a preheated oven (180-200ºC) and bake for 30-40 minutes.

5. Serve the beans warm.

PALIKARIA – FOTOKOLYVA
(MIXED LEGUGES)
Serves 8

INGREDIENTS

1 cup whole wheat

1 cup chick-peas

1 cup lima beans

1 cup green peas

1 cup black-eyed peas

olive oil

1 lemon, the juice

salt

Topping (optional)

dill, finely chopped

spring onion, finely chopped

DIRECTIONS

1. Soak the legumes overnight in as many bowls of water as the kinds of legumes mentioned in the recipe.

2. Heat water in a casserole and then boil the legumes as follows: first add the wheat and boil it for 20 minutes, then add the beans, chick-peas and green peas and boil for 30 more minutes.

3. Strain the legumes when they are half done. Heat fresh water again; add the legumes and boil them until done. The change and use of warm water keeps the legumes tender.

4. Place the mixed legumes in a large dish, season them with salt and sprinkle with a lot of olive oil and lemon juice.

LIMA BEANS IN THE OVEN
Serves 8

INGREDIENTS

1 cup common olive oil

2 cups lima beans (previously soaked for 7-8 hours)

2 onions, finely chopped

1 bunch celery, finely chopped

2 cloves garlic, finely sliced

1 teaspoon tomato paste

1 large tomato, mashed

1 medium-sized tomato, finely sliced

1 teaspoon oregano

3-4 drops of lemon juice

1 teaspoon sugar

salt & pepper to taste

DIRECTIONS

1. Boil the beans in a lot of water for 35 minutes and drain them through a colander.

2. Pour the olive oil in a casserole; heat it to sauté the onion and garlic for 3-4 minutes. Add the tomato, tomato paste (previously dissolved in a cup of water), all the spices, sugar and lemon juice. Stir and add one more cup of water. Cover the casserole and simmer for 15-20 minutes.

3. Spread the lima bean in a baking/fire-proof (pyrex) dish and pour the sauce over the beans. Arrange the tomato slices on top and sprinkle with a little pepper. Bake in a preheated oven at 180ºC for 30-40 minutes.

CHICK-PEAS IN BIGARADE ORANGE JUICE

Serves 8

INGREDIENTS

3 cups chick-peas

2 large onions, finely chopped

1 cup olive oil

1 water glass bigarade orange juice

1 tablespoon flour

1 bay leaf

1 teaspoon salt

1 teaspoon cumin

DIRECTIONS

1. Soak the chick-peas in a bowl of water overnight. The following day boil them in a pot with five cups of water.

2. When the chick-peas are done, add the olive oil, onions, salt and let them boil at 100ºC for 20 more minutes.

3. Dissolve the flour in the bigarade juice and add the mixture to the pot with the chick-peas. Stir and add the cumin and bay leaf. Cover the pot; turn off heat and let the pot on the ring for 8 minutes before serving.

BROAD BEANS PUREE IN OLIVE OIL

Serves 8

This is a very common dish topped with finely chopped onion and sardines on the side.

INGREDIENTS

1 cup olive oil

2 cups dry broad beans, large

1 large onion, finely chopped

3-4 drops of lemon juice

salt to taste

DIRECTIONS

1. Soak the beans in water overnight and boil them for 20 minutes in a lot of water the following day. Strain and let them cool down slightly.

2. Transfer the broad beans into another casserole, add enough water to top them up and boil them for 10 more minutes, without the lid on. Strain again the let them cool down completely.

3. Shell the broad beans and place them in a pot with two cups of water. Season them with a little salt. Cook the broad beans, stirring frequently with a wooden ladle, until they absorb all liquids and turn into puree. Stir more and/or add a little water to achieve the puree effect.

4. Serve the puree warm in little dishes. Pour a tablespoon of olive oil over the puree, also, a drop of lemon juice and sprinkle with chopped onion.

LENTIL SOUP

Serves 6

INGREDIENTS

2 cups lentils

3 large and ripe tomatoes, grated

2 cloves garlic, thinly sliced

2 bay leaves

1 large onion, finely chopped

2 carrots, cleaned and thinly sliced

3-4 tablespoons vinegar from red wine

3/4 cup olive oil

salt and pepper to taste

vinegar to top

DIRECTIONS

1. Clean the lentils and boil them in a pot with water for 3 minutes, then drain. Again, boil them in fresh water for 20 minutes approximately.

2. Add the garlic, onion, carrots and bay leaf into the pot and continue cooking. Taste to see if the lentils are almost done, then add the tomato, olive oil, pepper and salt. Continue cooking until you get a thick soup.

3. Turn off heat and sprinkle each serving with a little vinegar.

BLACK-EYED BEANS WITH FENNEL & SPINACH

Serves 8

INGREDIENTS

2 cups black-eyed beans

2 ripe tomatoes, finely chopped

1 cup olive oil

2 tablespoons fennel, finely chopped

1 cup spinach, finely chopped

salt and pepper to taste

DIRECTIONS

1. Place the beans in little water for 10 minutes before cooking them. Transfer the beans in a pot with boiling water and let them boil for 25 minutes approximately. Then remove them using a perforated spoon and transfer them into a colander to drain well.

2. Use a casserole to sauté the onion and fennels with the spinach in olive oil. Add one cup of water and cook for 20 minutes. Add the beans, tomatoes, salt, pepper and a little water into the casserole. Simmer for 20 more minutes. Serve warm or at room temperature.

SPLIT PEAS (*FAVA*) BURGERS

Serves 6

INGREDIENTS

2 cups split peas (previously cooked and pureed (fava))

1 teaspoon fresh mint, finely chopped

2 tablespoons fine semolina

1 cup olive oil

salt & pepper to taste

DIRECTIONS

1. Prepare the split peas puree (fava) and store it in the refrigerator. 24 hours later empty the fava puree in a large bowl.

2. Into the same bowl you add the onion, mint, semolina, salt & pepper. Mix the ingredients by hand to a homogenous pulp.

3. Knead the mixture into small balls, the size of a large walnut and then press each ball between your palms to flatten it into a burger. When done, place the flattened burgers into the fridge for an hour.

4. In a non-stick frying pan heat olive oil. Remove the burgers from the fridge and place them into the pan using a spatula. Fry the burgers over high temperature until golden brown on both sides.

5. When the burgers are done, remove them with a perforated spatula and place them on a platter lined with kitchen paper. Serve them warm.

SPLIT PEAS, PUREE
Serves 8-10

INGREDIENTS

1/2 kg split peas

1 small onion, finely chopped

little salt

little olive oil

little lemon juice

DIRECTIONS

1. You can buy split peas in bulk or in standard packets. In any case, rinse the split peas under tap water and drain them. Bring them to a boil in a pot with 1 lt of salted water. Strain and rinse under tap water.

2. Replace the split peas into the pot with 1 lt of fresh water. Boil them until they absorb all water. Before you take the pot off the ring, add the onion and salt.

3. When the split peas are done, transfer them into a mixer bowl and run the mixer to make a paste out of the split peas (fava). Serve the fava topped with a little olive oil and lemon juice.

4. (Optional: you may sprinkle the fava servings with finely chopped onion and/or dill.)

Rice – Gruel – Xynochondros

The "cracked" wheat, either in its simple form (as it comes out of the old hand-mill) or processed to semolina, or boiled and ground to gruel, or mixed with sweet or sour milk, yoghurt, hebrs or vegetables, has been one of the most important meals in the broader Mediterranean and Balkan regions for thousands of years.

In fact, the first written testimonies for the use of the coarsely ground wheat (Gk. *hontros*) come from Dioscurides (c. 512 AD), Oreivasios (c. 4th AD) and Athenaeus (c. 200 AD). Food writer and historian Charles Perry claims that the word "*tarkahana*" first appeared in a Persian poem of the 14th or 15th century. However, no such word ever came up in ancient Greek texts. Nevertheless, P. Genadios (1950) claims that *trachanas* (or *xynohondros* = Wheat soup with goat's sour milk) is made from boiled milk and hondros (wheat boiled in milk) and probably is the "tragos" of the ancient Greeks.

Mr. Michalis Kopidakis, professor at the University of Athens, claims the same in his book "Praise to Wine / Oenon Epaeno". To support P. Genadios' claim, the professor quotes Hesiod, "*Μάζα τ' αλμογαίη γάλα τ' αίγων σβεννυμενάων*", which he translated as follows: "... trachana and the milk from goats that have stopped feeding their kids".

In their texts, *Dioscurides* and *Oreivasios* made long references to the nutritional value of hondros and tragos. Athenaeus provides us with bread-making recipes involving the addition of coarsely ground wheat (*hondritis* bread), as well as references to pastries and salty meals made from coarsely ground wheat or barley.

XYNOCHONDROS

This is made mainly in Crete, as well as in Turkey, Syria and Lebanon. If you visit Crete in the summer and drive in the hinterland, your eyes may catch a glimpse of xynochondros basking in the sun on flat roofs in the form of a collection of oblong or round lumps. The meal *xynochondros* is a mixture of cracked wheat, gruel, thin and soured milk resembling in constitution a soup or cream. Xynochondros is made to look more like a small, oblong "meat ball" and. while still fresh, is spread on a clean cloth and put under the sun to dry. *Xynochondros* is ready to cook when it has lost 85% of its liquids, in which case it reduces in volume and then stored. If *xynochondros* is dried well, it can last for 3-4 years, otherwise mould appears.

The *xynochondros* is also used as condiment (instead of butter) with the aim to add particular taste to meat. It is quit nourishing this way. Fresh *xynochondros* may be consumed before it dries completely. It is usually accompanied with sweet grapes.

XYNOCHONDROS

Serves 6-8

INGREDIENTS

4kg fresh milk

3 cups ground wheat or gruel

1 1/2 tablespoons salt

1/2 lemon, the juice

2 tablespoons olive oil

DIRECTIONS

1. For a period of 3-4 days pour 1lt of milk in a large bowl per day to turn it sour. Stir occasionally.

2. Use a large pot to heat the sour milk and the lemon juice. Before it comes to the boil, add the wheat. Lower heat and cook for 30 minutes, but stir continuously, so that the wheat does not stick to the pot.

3. Serve the *xynochondros* warm or at room temperature.

AUBERGINES WITH *XYNOCHONDROS*

Serves 6-8

INGREDIENTS

8 aubergines, long type

2 onions, finely chopped

1 bunch parsley, finely chopped

2 ripe tomatoes

1 cup olive oil

1 cup *xynochondros*

DIRECTIONS

1. Score the aubergines length-wise and place them in a bowl with two tablespoons of sugar.

2. Use a large pot to sauté the onions in olive oil and add the parsley when the onions turn translucent.

3. Rinse the aubergines under tap water and arrange them in the pot.

4. Use a bowl to coarsely grate the tomato. Add the *xynochondros* in this bowl to soften for 7 minutes and then add this mixture into the pot with the aubergines.

5. Cover the pot and cook over moderate heat for 40 minutes, occasionally shaking the pot by the handle(s) to mix the ingredients well.

XYNOCHONDROS SOUP WITH CHICK-PEAS

Serves 8

INGREDIENTS

1 1/2 cups chick-peas (soaked in
cold water for 8 hours)
1 cup *xynochondros*
1 large onion, finely chopped
3/4 cup olive oil
1 medium tomato, skinned
3/4 lemon, the juice
salt and pepper

DIRECTIONS

1. Pour the olive oil in a pot and heat it (do not burn!). Add the onion to
sauté for 3-4 minutes, until it becomes translucent.
2. Drain the chick-peas and sauté them with the onion. Add 3/4 lt of water
and cover the pot to simmer the meal for 40-45 minutes – pot covered with
its lid.
3. Soak the xynochondros in 1 1/2 cups of water. Add the *xynochondros* to
the chick-peas, the tomato and little salt. Stir to mix the ingredients and
continue cooking for 20-25 minutes without the lid on the pot.
4. Then add the lemon juice and a little pepper. Serve the soup warm.

HONDROS w. ONION, POTATO, MARROW

Serves 6-8

INGREDIENTS

2 cups hondros (cracked wheat
or gruel)
1 cup olive oil
1 large onion, finely chopped
1 medium tomato, finely
chopped
1 large potato, peeled and
cubed
1 medium marrow, chopped to
medium cubes
salt & pepper

DIRECTIONS

1. Sauté the onion in the olive oil to lightly brown. Add the tomato and
simmer for 3-4 minutes. Add 9 cups of water and let it come to the boil.
2. Then add the hondros, stir and season with salt and pepper. Lower heat
(stir the hondros, otherwise it will stick to the sides of the cooking vessel) and
simmer for 40 minutes. Add the potatoes and continue cooking for 10 more
minutes. Finally, add the marrow, a little salt and simmer for 15 minutes more.
3. Remove pot from heat and cover it with a cotton cloth for 10 minutes
before serving. Serve with a lot of pepper.

PILAF WITH AUBERGINES AND MINT

Serves 6-8

INGREDIENTS

1kg long aubergines, chopped

1 1/2 cups rice

1 large onion, finely grated

1 large tomato, cubed

1 tablespoon mint, fresh and chopped

1 tablespoon salt

1 cup olive oil

freshly ground pepper

DIRECTIONS

1. Add the aubergines in a lot of salted water and let them stand for one hour.

2. Use a large pot to lightly sauté the onion in the olive oil. Add the aubergines, stir and lower heat to simmer for 3-4 minutes. Add the tomato and 4 cups of water to cook for 7 more minutes. Do not cover the pot.

3. Add 5 more cups of water and bring it to the boil. Add the rice to simmer for 20 minutes. Remove the pot from heat, add the mint and stir lightly. Cover the pot with a cotton cloth and let it stand for 10-20 minutes for the aubergine-pilaf to absorb the liquids.

4. Serve warm with a lot of pepper.

TOMATO-RICE WITH GRAPES

Serves 6

INGREDIENTS

1 cup rice

1 cup tomato juice

3/4 cup olive oil

1 small onion, finely chopped

2 cups water

salt & pepper

DIRECTIONS

1. Use a pot to sauté the onion in the olive oil. Add 2 cups of water, the tomato juice, salt and bring all to the boil.

2. Add the rice, stir and bring all to the boil for three minutes. Then lower heat and cover the pot to simmer. Stir occasionally and let the meal absorb almost all of its juices.

3. When the rice is done, remove pot from the heat and cover it with a cotton cloth for 10 minutes.

4. Serve warm; sprinkle with a lot of pepper and a few grapes.

SPINACH-RICE

Serves 6-8

INGREDIENTS

1kg spinach

2 ripe tomatoes, peeled and finely chopped

1 large onion, finely chopped

3 spring onions, chopped

1 cup parsley

2 cups rice

1/2 teaspoon cumin (optional)

salt & pepper

DIRECTIONS

1. Clean spinach (remove yellow/dry leaves) and rinse it in a large bowl under tap water.

2. Use a large pot to sauté the onions in the olive oil. Add the spinach, tomato, parsley and simmer for 12–15 minutes without adding any water.

3. Use a perforated spatula to transfer the mixture from the pot to the large plate, but leave a thin layer of spinach at the bottom of the pot.

4. On top of the bottom layer of spinach spread a portion of the rice, then place another layer of spinach, then rice again, until you have exhausted the ingredients. Add in the spices in quantities fitting your taste and six cups of water (1cup rice over 3cups water). Cook the spinach over moderate heat for 20 minutes.

5. When done, remove the pot from heat and cover it with a cotton cloth for 10 minutes before serving. Spinach-rice is usually thinner than pilaf.

Snails of Crete: a healthy delicacy

When the English traveler Robert Pashley visited Crete in 1881, he spent some time with the locals in an effort to learn more about their daily customs and diet. He noted the following in his diary: "In the evening captain Menas and his friends had snails for dinner. It was a delicious and sumptuous meal that Cretans and other Greeks enjoy even at periods of fasting. The snails of Crete are renowned in the entire East and constitute the most significant export product of the island." For Cretans, the snails were a staple until a few decades ago, as much as bread, olive oil and wine.

SNAILS AND HISTORY

Snails have been a favourite delicacy for Cretans for the last 3000 years. Evidence for this are the shells found in numerous clay jars of the Minoan period in Santorini. This should not come as a surprise, since the gathering and maintenance of snails does not require much effort.

These little terrestrial gastropod mollusks have a tasty flesh that has remained consistent through the ages. Unfortunately for them, so has the interest of the people of Crete and Greece. The Cretans go "snailing" with the first rains of the season, when the new grass starts to nudge out of the soil. As they have been collecting and cooking snails for hundreds of years, Cretans have concocted scores of recipes for snail dishes. The Portuguese may boast of one thousand ways of cooking cod, but the Cretans are equally proud of their imagination in cooking snails in as many ways, or even more.

Snails and health

Following a biological investigation of snails, Serge Renault found that their fatty constituents are similar to the olive oil. This means that if one consumes snails twice a week, as Cretans do, then one receives the required elements that shield the heart from diseases or even prevent cancer growths. Snails are rich in proteins, precious minerals and low in fats (an average serving of snails, approx. 7 snails, provides 4 times less fat than a serving of beef).

The nutritional value of snails is also corroborated by author Mr. Stelios Markakis, in his book "Snails in the Greek and European kitchen". He says that snails contain proteins whose amino acids promote health, while their content in bacteria is ten times less than those found in meat.

HOW TO CLEAN SNAILS

You need a little sharp knife to remove the membrane at the opening of the shell and scrape off any dirt on the shell. Rinse snails well under tap water then place them in salted water for 4-5 minutes. Drain and then set them aside, or put them in the freezer.

SNAILS IN ROSEMARY

Serves 4

INGREDIENTS

20 snails in their shells

1/2 cup olive oil

2 tsp salt

3 tbsp strong, red vinegar

1 tsp rosemary

DIRECTIONS

1. Wash the snails thoroughly in a lot of lukewarm water. Pick a pointed knife and remove the membranes from the shell openings (face), if necessary.

2. Place a non-stick frying pan on oven ring and sprinkle its bottom with 1 tablespoon of salt. Place each snail face down in the pan and fry without stirring at high temperature for 4-5 minutes. Sprinkle the rest of the salt over snails and add the olive oil. Continue frying at moderate temperature for another 5-6 minutes.

3. Pick a fork and stir snails in the pan, sprinkle with rosemary and pour the vinegar all over the snails. Let the snails "boil" in vinegar for 1-2 minutes and then remove the frying pan from the oven ring. Serve snails hot in their juice.

HONDROS (GRUEL) WITH SNAILS

Serves 7-8

INGREDIENTS

1/2 kg gruel (or frumenty)

1/2 kg snails

1/2 -1 cup olive oil

1/2 kg tomatoes

1 onion, finely chopped

salt & pepper

DIRECTIONS

1. In a pot boil the snails for 2-3 minutes. Drain and rinse them under tap water. Transfer them into a pot with olive oil and sauté them with the onion. Season with the salt and pepper, add the tomato and cook them until done. To test if the snails are done, use of fork and try to poke one snail out of its shell. If it comes out entirely, not cut in half, you need to cook them more.

2. Remove snails from the pot using a perforated spoon; add 4 cups of water and bring it to the boil, then add the gruel.

3. Stir well, until the gruel thickens and then add the snails to boil for 3-4 minutes.

4. Turn off heat; remove pot from the ring and let it rest for 5-10 minutes. Serve the snails with a little pepper.

SNAILS WITH TOMATO AND BAY LEAF

Serves 6

INGREDIENTS

1/2 kg snails

4-5 tomatoes, ripe and chopped

1 large onion, finely chopped

1 bay leaf

1/2 tablespoon cumin

Guinea pepper, 2 grains

Salt & pepper

DIRECTIONS

1. Clean and wash the snails well, as per previous instructions. Boil the snails in a pot for 10 minutes and then drain them.

2. Use a second pot to sauté the onion in olive oil. Add the tomatoes, salt, spices, pepper and bay leaf and simmer until the sauce forms.

3. When the sauce is ready, add the snails and let the meal cook over moderate heat for 15 more minutes. Serve warm or at rooms temperature.

SNAILS MONASTERY STYLE

Serves 6

INGREDIENTS

20-30 snails

1 medium lemon, the juice

1 tablespoon flour

1 1/2 tablespoon olive oil

1/2 teaspoon oregano

1 teaspoon salt

DIRECTIONS

1. Clean and wash the snails as per above instructions. Use a pot to boil the snails in salted water for 8 minutes. Drain and add one glass of fresh water into the same pot, the salt, olive oil and oregano.

2. Boil the snails for 3 minutes and add the flour (dissolved in the lemon juice). Stir and turn off heat. Let the pot rest on the ring for 10 minutes, then remove from the ring and serve.

SNAILS WITH POTATOES, GARLIC AND TOMATO

Serves 6-8

INGREDIENTS

30-40 snails

2 potatoes, large and cut to 4 pcs

4 tomatoes, small and cut to 4 pcs

6 cloves garlic

1 cup olive oil

DIRECTIONS

1. Clean and wash the snails well – remove membranes and scrape off dirt on the shells. Boil them for 10 minutes and set them aside.

2. Use a second pot to boil the cut potatoes and tomatoes for 30 minutes. Ten minutes before you remove this pot from heat, add the snails and garlic.

3. Place the meal in a large plate; pour the olive oil raw and season with salt.

"ST. GEORGE'S" OMELET

Serves 6

INGREDIENTS

8 eggs

1 teaspoon fresh mint, finely chopped

4 tablespoons goat's cheese, hard and grated

1 1/2 tablespoons flour

2 tablespoons olive oil

salt & pepper

DIRECTIONS

1. Place the finely chopped mint into a deep dish, add the cheese, flour, salt & pepper and mix well.

2. Use a bowl to whisk the eggs and gradually add the above mixture stirring all the while to get a smooth, porridge-like mixture.

3. Heat olive oil in a frying pan and pour in the mixture. Let the omelet cook from one side. Use a long spatula to detach the omelet from the sides of the pan.

4. Drain most of the olive oil from the pan and turn the omelet over using a large, flat dish. Continue frying over lower heat for 7 more minutes, but turn the omelet over 4-5 times in the while.

OMELET WITH COURGETTES, TOMATOES & FETA CHEESE

Serves 6

INGREDIENTS

2 medium-sized tomatoes, ripe and
finely chopped

2 medium-sized courgettes, sliced

150gr feta cheese, cubed

6 eggs

4 tablespoons olive oil

salt & pepper to taste

DIRECTIONS

1. Fry the courgettes in olive oil, then
strain, add the tomatoes and stir to
simmer for 7-8 minutes.

2. Add the eggs (whisked and
seasoned with salt & pepper) mixed
with the feta cheese.

3. Fry over low heat and stir 2-3 times
using a wooden ladle.

Pies – *Bourekia*
(Patties)

CRETAN PIES

Pies are a typical snack or meal in the Cretan and Greek cuisine and a worthy representative of a long tradition rooted in the remote past. The basic ingredients in the making of pies are phyllos of dough, herbs, garden vegetables and olive oil. Other ingredients are also used: cheese, eggs and milk. Pies are a tasty expression of the gastronomic spirit – practical and Spartan. Pie varieties are endless, each the result of imagination, skill and local ingredients.

The ancient Greeks made their bread / pies on a slate of stone which they heated on open fire or on a portable or fixed semi-circular oven (klivanos). They cupped the bread with cinder or hot adobe tiles to cook the top part of the bread. Bread cooked on heated slates looked like pies or cakes and referred to as *'plakitis'* or *'plakous'*. This mode of cooking bread continued through the Byzantine period from 700-1200 A.D. and the descriptive terms used for this kind of bread were plakisti or plakopita or ceramopita.

The term pita (pie/cake) first appeared in 12th c. texts and is still used. In his poems Theodore the Forerunner, 12th c. AD., uses the term ceramopita, which is a simple pie in the skillet. In Byzantine glossaries (e.g. Meoursios') the plakopita is associated with a version of plakountas. The same is true in 14th century texts (The Life of Maximus the Athonite). These pies or cakes were mostly round in form, but also elongated or triangular and made from two or more phyllos of dough. The filling used was made from an assortment of cheeses, spices, sesame, dill, almonds, nuts and semolina. We now know that the Greeks differentiated their bread by adding to the dough various herbs, such as parsley and mint and peppermint.

KINDS OF PIES

Currently, pies are made from phyllo dough or porridge and stuffed with various ingredients. Cretan pies are distinguished in terms of the variety of ingredients, shape

and cooking modes. They can be fried in generous quantities of olive oil, baked in the oven or on scalding hot slates (*Sfakiaes pites*).

THE *PHYLLO*

The making of phyllo at home requires considerable skill and as a rule was practiced by women in Crete. This skill ascribed an admirable social status to women, being also part of a ritual that was later incorporated into the Christian Orthodox faith. In particular, before kneading bread the women would prostrate, cross themselves, and pray. The basic ingredients for the phyllo are dough (from wheat or corn), olive oil, salt and water. Other ingredients included eggs, milk, yogurt and yeast. The dough is kneaded by bare hands and then rolled out to paper thin layers. For roller the women used a cylindrical stick the name of which varied from location to location. Some phyllo layers were made entirely by hand (as in agnopites, Sfakianes, neropites) or by the short and thick stem of a reed.

FILLING

Pies are filled with a wide range of ingredients, which differ from one location to another on the island of Crete. The basic ingredients used for filling are resourced locally. In meat pies, for example, pork or lamb combines with cheese or rice. There are pies whose basic ingredients are herbs or vegetables (courgettes, sweet pumpkin, potatoes and goat cheese).

Pies are also distinguished in terms of ingredient proportions, which vary from location to location and household to household. This liberal use of ingredients and proportions of the same resulted in a wide variety of delicious pies, but it is also indicative of the local crops, the economic status of the region and families, and the skills and imagination of the women who make these pies.

SPINACH PIE

INGREDIENTS

Phyllo:

1 cup virgin olive oil

2 eggs

1 teaspoon salt

1 1/2 cups milk

700gr flour, soft

the yolk from one egg

1 cup sesame

Filling:

3 tablespoons extra virgin olive oil

1kg spinach, finely chopped

1 bunch parsley, finely chopped

8 spring onions (the green tender stems only), finely chopped

2 tablespoons finely chopped mint

2 cups feta cheese, crumbled

salt and pepper to taste

DIRECTIONS

1. Use a blender to mix the olive oil, milk, salt and two cups of flour. Switch to high speed; add the flour little by little to get a smooth paste that does not stick to the sides of the blender bowl. Check thickness by hand. Remove the mixture from the blender bowl and knead it on a floured surface for 4-5 minutes. Cover the dough with a cotton towel and let it rest and proceed with the filling.

2. Toss the chopped spinach and parsley into a large bowl. Rub the green mixture between your palms to 'shrivel' and season it with salt. Add the onions, mint, pepper and feta cheese.

3. Divide the dough in two portions. Pick one portion and roll it out into a phyllo on a floured surface. The area or diameter of your phyllo should be greater/longer than the area or the diameter of your baking pan. Grease the bottom of the pan and place the phyllo so that its perimeter extends a little over the rim of your pan. Spread the filling over the phyllo; use a spoon to make an even surface of the filling. Place a second phyllo on top of the filling and seal the filling by pressing the perimeters of the phyllos together.

4. Whisk the egg yolk and brush the pie with it. Sprinkle the pie with the sesame and bake at 180ºC for 40-45 minutes. Let the pie cool down before cutting it. Serve warm or at room temperature.

OVEN PIES STUFFED WITH CHEESE

Serves 10

INGREDIENTS

1 cup milk

6 eggs

1 cup butter (at room temperature)

1/2 teaspoon ammonia

1 tablespoon baking powder

1 tablespoon sugar

700–800gr flour, hard

cheese filling:

1kg ricotta or feta cheese

2 eggs

1 tablespoon sugar

1 teaspoon cinnamon

DIRECTIONS

1. Use a bowl to mix the salt, baking powder and flour. Make a well in the center of the mixture and add the eggs, butter, ammonia (dissolved in lukewarm milk). Start kneading with your hands until you get homogenous and rather hard dough. Cover the dough with a wet (but strained) cotton cloth and let it rest for 20–30 minutes.

2. Cheese filling: mix the cheese with the eggs, sugar and cinnamon.

3. Divide the dough into ten (10) balls. Roll each ball out to a thin sheet and take out circular cuts using a saucer, approx. 15 cm in diameter. Place a tablespoon of filling in the middle of each cut and fold the cut dough to a crescent shape.

4. Place crescents into a greased baking dish, brush them with a little whisked egg and cook in a preheated over at 180ºC for 40-45 minutes. Serve pies warm or at room temperature.

MYRTLE SCENTED SPINACH-KALITSOUNIA PIES

30 pieces

INGREDIENTS

Phyllo:

1kg soft flour

2 glasses of lukewarm water

4 tablespoons raki / grap

4 tablespoons olive oil

1 teaspoon salt

2 eggs, for brushing

sesame to sprinkle

2-3 myrtle sprigs

Filling:

2kg spinach

6 spring onions, finely chopped

4 tablespoons olive oil

3 bunches spearmint, finely chopped

1kg ricotta

1/2 kg feta cheese

1/2 kg crème fraiche

4 tablespoons flour

salt and pepper to taste

DIRECTIONS

1. Clean, wash and strain the spinach. Chop and sauté it with the onions in olive oil for 3 minutes.

2. Strain the spinach again and place it in a bowl. Add the spearmint, ricotta, feta, flour, salt and pepper. Mix all ingredients very well.

3. Make the phyllo: mix the flour with the water, raki/grap, olive oil and salt. Knead very well to get a lump that does not stick to your hands – correct with more flour if it does. Use a kneading board to roll the dough lumps out into medium thickness sheets 8x8 cm.

4. Cut out square pieces (approx. 6 x 6 cm) of phyllo and place 2 tablespoons of filling in the middle of each square. Moisten the edges of the phyllo squares and raise the corners bringing them almost half way to the center. Brush the stuffed phyllo squares (kalitsounia) with your whisked eggs and sprinkle with the sesame.

5. Place the kalitsounia into a large, greased baking pan and bake in a preheated oven at 200ºC for 20-25 minutes. In the meanwhile arrange the myrtle sprigs in a large bowl to let the kalitsounia rest there for sometime to pick up the aroma.

HANIOTIKO BOUREKI

Serves 8

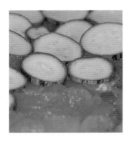

INGREDIENTS

1 1/2 courgettes or pumpkin

4 medium-sized potatoes

1gk ricotta or soft goat's cheese

1/2 kg hard feta, grated

1 cup strained yogurt

2 medium-sized tomatoes, finely chopped

1 tablespoon fresh mint, finely chopped

4 tablespoons crème fraiche

3 tablespoons olive oil

2 cups flour

1 tablespoon sesame

very little salt

pepper

DIRECTIONS

1. Thinly slice the courgettes and potatoes, toss them in a large bowl and sprinkle them with salt. Add the finely chopped tomatoes, mint, half of all cheese quantities (previously mixed), crème fraiche, olive oil, pepper and 1 1/2 cups flour. Stir vigorously by hand.

2. Grease the bottom of a baking pan and spread the mixture using a spatula. Do the same with the cheeses on the mixture and sprinkle with any flour left over and with the sesame.

3. Insert the pan in a preheated oven and bake at 200ºC for 45 minutes. Cover the pan with aluminum foil and cook at 150ºC for 30 more minutes. Serve the boureki at room temperature or cold.

HERB PIES (*CHORTOPITES*)
30 pieces

INGREDIENTS

Phyllo:

1kg hard flour

1/2 cup raki

salt, a shot

lukewarm water

3 tablespoons olive oil

Filling:

1kg spinach, finely chopped

1 fennel root, chopped

1 cup celery, finely chopped

6 spring onions, finely chopped

1 tablespoon olive oil

1/2 teaspoon pepper

1 teaspoon cumin

salt to taste

olive oil for frying

DIRECTIONS

1. Clean, wash and chop the herbs/greens, but to do not let them drain completely. Use a pot to sauté the spring onions in olive oil for 2–3 minutes. Add the herbs/greens in the pot; stir, sprinkle with salt, lower heat and cover the pot with its lid. Simmer the ingredients for 20-30 minutes. Add a little water if necessary. Then add the cumin, pepper and stir vigorously.

2. Transfer the herbs/greens into a colander to strain completely – use a spatula to apply a little pressure, and allow them to cool down completely.

3. Make dough using the phyllo ingredients. Your dough should be tender and not too thin or runny. Cover the dough with a cotton towel and let it rest for an hour.

4. Pick a lump of dough and roll it out into phyllos (1-2 cm thick); then using a saucer (8-9 cm in diameter) stamp out phyllo disks. Place a little filling in the middle of each disk using a fork and fold disks to crescent shape. Press the crescent perimeter with the back of the fork to secure the filling.

5. Heat olive oil in a skillet to fry the pies. As soon as pies are golden brown remove them using a perforated spoon and place them on kitchen paper. Serve them warm.

BOUREKAKIA (LITTLE CUSTARD PIES)
30-40 pieces

INGREDIENTS

2 cups sour *myzithra*

3 cups sweet *myzithra* or *ricotta*

3 eggs

1 teaspoon cinnamon

3 tablespoons honey

1 tablespoon butter

1 packet phyllo sheets

Syrup:

2 cups sugar

1 cup water

the juice from one lemon

1 cinnamon stick

DIRECTIONS

1. Mix all of the myzithra (sour & sweet), eggs, cinnamon and honey in a bowl. This is your filling.

2. Cut the phyllo sheets to 20x8 cm in dimensions and grease (butter) them lightly. Place 2-3 phyllos on top of each other and place 1 tablespoon from the myzithra filling in the center of the phyllo layers. Turn the sides in and roll. Repeat the process until you have exhausted the filling and phyllos. Place the custard pies in a baking dish and bake at 180ºC for 25-30 minutes, until golden brown.

3. In the meanwhile prepare the syrup and let it cool down. Remove the baking dish with the pies from the oven, pour the syrup over and let it sip into the pies before serving.

MEAT PIE WITH YOGHURT

Serves 10

INGREDIENTS

Phyllo:
1/2 kg yoghurt
1/4 kg butter
1 sachet yeast
1/2 teaspoon soda
1 egg
sesame (to top)
salt to taste
flour (as much as it takes)

Filling:
1 1/2 kg meat, young lamb
1/2 kg ricotta
1/2 kg gruyere, grated
2 tablespoons crème fraiche
1/2 cup meat stock
5 spearmint leaves, finely chopped
pepper to taste

DIRECTIONS

1. Use a large bowl to dissolve the yoghurt and butter in a little lukewarm water. Add the flour, yeast and a little salt. Mix the ingredients with your hands until the dough forms.

2. Flour a smooth surface and knead the dough, adding as much flour as it takes to get smooth dough that does not stick to your hands. Place the dough lump on grease paper and cover it with a cotton towel. Let it stand to rise for 45 minutes approximately.

3. Boil the meat for 40 minutes and then let it cool down. Remove bones and cut meat to little pieces.

4. Use a bowl to mix the cheeses, the meat, spearmint, meat stock and pepper. Grease a large, removable-bottom pan.

5. Divide the dough in two lumps. Over a floured surface roll out one lump into a phyllo 30 cm in diameter. Place this phyllo at the bottom of the tin with its perimeter hanging out the rim of the tin. Add in and spread out evenly the filling of cheese and meat.

6. Roll out the other lump of dough – a little smaller this time – and use it to cover the pie. Use your fingers to tuck in the outer perimeter of the bottom phyllo onto the perimeter of the top phyllo to seal the pie. Cover with a cotton towel for 10 minutes.

7. Preheat oven at 180ºC. Brush the top of the pie with whisked egg and sprinkle with a lot of sesame. Bake at 100ºC for 60 minutes. Let the pie cool down for 20 minutes before serving.

SARIKOPITES (pies)
30 pieces

INGREDIENTS
Phyllo
1/2 kg hard flour
1/2 teaspoon salt
3 tablespoons olive oil
1 lemon, the juice of
1-2 cups lukewarm water
olive oil for frying

Filling:
1/2 sour goat's cheese, soft
honey (for topping, optional)

DIRECTIONS
1. Use a large bowl to pour in the flour. Make a well in the center of the flour 'mount' and pour in the olive oil, lemon juice, the lukewarm water (slowly), and sprinkle with the salt. Start kneading with your hands until you get a homogenous and smooth dough, adding flour or water to achieve the desired result.

2. Make five (5) small balls out of the dough. Flour a smooth surface and roll out one of the balls into a paper-thin, rectangular phyllo (not transparent). Cut the phyllo into strips, 7-9 cm wide and 30 cm long. Spread the cheese along the first strip leaving an empty space, 3-4 cm, from both ends of the strip. Roll the strip, as you would a cigarette, by raising and rolling in one of the long sides of the strip. Now, the stuffed strip looks more like a cord. Make a loose coil out of this cord. Repeat the process using the rest of the dough balls.

3. Pour a lot of olive in a frying pan, enough to top the coils and fry them. When the pies are done, transfer them on a plate lined with kitchen paper. Serve them with a lot of honey on top.

DEVOTIONAL BREAD

4-5 loaves

INGREDIENTS

2kg white flour

2 tablespoons baking powder

3 pieces mastic, crashed

1 teaspoon cinnamon, grated

1 teaspoon cloves, crashed

4 lemon leaves

4 pelargonium leaves

1 kg sugar

1 cup olive oil

150gr yeast

DIRECTIONS

1. Dissolve the yeast in two cups of lukewarm water; add this into a large bowl with the olive oil, cinnamon, cloves, mastic and sugar. This is your mixture.

2. Boil the lemon and pelargonium leaves into a pot with 1/2 a litter of water for 4 minutes. Allow the juice to reach a lukewarm temperature. Add the flour into the mixture in the bowl and the juice little by little.

3. Start kneading using your hands, but occasionally dip your hands in a dish with olive oil.

4. At some time you will get fluffy dough that does not stick to the sides of the bowl. Pick up the dough lump and put it aside on a safe and warm surface in your kitchen. Cover the dough with a cotton cloth and small blanket and let it rise for about 2-3 hours.

5. When the dough has risen, divide it into 4-5 lumps and knead equivalent loaves of bread per each lump. Cover the loaves again to let them rise again.

6. Before you bake the loaves of bread, brush them with sugar-water. Place the loaves in a baking dish (allow space for the loaves to expand), brush them with a little olive oil and bake them at 180ºC for 45-50 minutes.

RAISIN BREAD WITH ORANGE

3 oblong loaves

INGREDIENTS

1 kg hard flour

350gr raisins

3 tablespoons orange rind, grated

3 teaspoons yeast

150gr sugar

1 teaspoon salt

3/4 glass milk, lukewarm

3 tablespoons olive oil

DIRECTIONS

1. Pour the milk in a bowl to dissolve the yeast; add one teaspoon of sugar; stir and cover the bowl to let the mixture foam.

2. Use a large bowl (or the bowl of a blender) to add the flour, sugar, salt and orange rind. Pour in the foamy yeast and start kneading (or run blender). Use as much warm water as it takes to get soft and elastic dough. When you are satisfied with the constitution of the dough, toss in the raisins (previously drenched with water and drained well). Knead the mixture to fold in the raisins, then add the olive oil and knead to let the dough absorb it.

3. Cover the dough and let it rest for 1/2 hour. Make two or three loaves and place them in long cake tins or on a large baking sheet lined with grease paper. Cover the tins/sheet with cotton cloth to let loaves rise and almost double in volume.

4. When the loaves have risen, brush them with the milk or whisked egg whites or lukewarm water. Before inserting them into the oven, pierce them on top at places (to prevent cracks) and bake in a preheated oven at 175ºC for one hour approximately.

Easter bread

All major religious festivals in Greece are part and parcel with devotional or ceremonial loaves of bread which, in addition to their gastronomic value, thrive in symbolism. Even to this day the Cretan Easter loaves symbolize benediction, fertility, rebirth of nature, etc. The tsoureki is a loaf of bread made from flour, milk, eggs, butter and yogurt. It is kneaded by women expert in making relief representations on top, e.g. daisies, birds, serpents, etc. Halved almonds are also stuck on top. The difference between the Easter bread and other decorative loaves of bread in Crete is the fact that the former incorporates a whole Easter (red) egg.

These bread items were offered to friends and/or relatives, while the number of Easter eggs marked the significance of the recipients to the person who made the offer. The same is true as regards the nature and complexity of the relief decorations on top of the bread. For example, animal representations (tortoises, snakes, lizards, partridges, etc.) were made on Easter bread intended for children (in the family or god-children).

EASTER ROUND BREAD
10 loaves

INGREDIENTS

3 kg flour (divide it into 2 equal portions)

1 kg sugar

1/2 kg yoghurt

4 eggs (room temperature)

1 cup olive oil

1 cup butter (room temperature)

150gr yeast

1 teaspoon cinnamon

1/2 teaspoon mastic, crashed with 1 tbsp sugar

1/2 teaspoon mahleb cherry, crashed

2 cups milk (lukewarm) for kneading

1 egg, the yolk (to brush)

DIRECTIONS

1. Use a large bowl to dissolve the yeast in two cups of lukewarm water. Work the mixture with your hands to dissolve it completely. Add 4-5 cups of flour (from one of the flour portions) in the bowl and use a spoon to mix it well, until it turns into a thick pulp. Cover the bowl with a cotton cloth and set it aside in your kitchen to double in volume (2 hours). You will also notice bubbles on top of the mixture. When you are satisfied with the volume increase, transfer the mixture into a larger bowl.

2. Use a smaller bowl to whisk the yogurt (or milk cream) with the sugar. Then add in the eggs (whisked), cinnamon, mastic, mahleb, olive oil and butter. Mix them well using your hands, until you get a homogenous mixture. Pour this mixture into the previous, large bowl and knead with your hands for 10 minutes. If you use a mixer, turn knob to middle position and run mixer for 5 minutes.

3. Add a cup of milk in the mixture and one and a half (1+1/2) kg flour (2nd portion). Start kneading using your hands, occasionally adding from the remaining flour, until you get firm dough that does not stick to the sides of the bowl. If the dough sticks to your hands, pick a little flour and rub it in your palms. Raise the dough lump from one side and sprinkle flour to the bottom and sides of the bowl. Continue kneading. Repeat the raising of dough and the sprinkling of flour once more. Continue kneading a little more; also clench your fists and punch hard on the dough for 2-3 minutes. Sprinkle the dough with a little milk and continue kneading for 3-4 minutes more.

4. Transfer the dough into a clean (lightly floured) bowl, cover with two cotton pieces of cloth and set aside in a warm place in your kitchen, until the dough doubles in volume (2-3 hours). As soon as the dough rises, place it on a flat surface (lightly floured) and knead it slowly. Divide the dough into 10 lumps and shape them to round loaves and/or make cylinders (7 cm in diameter), flatten (not much), place an Easter egg in the middle, bend sides around the egg and fold them (braid) on top of one another 2-3 times. Place the loaves on a lightly floured surface and cover them with two pieces of cotton cloth to rise.

5. To test whether the dough is ready for baking, press it a little using one of your fingers. If the pressure marks revert back, this implies that the dough has risen enough. Grease the bottom of baking sheets to place the loaves. Brush the loaves with whisked egg and insert the baking sheets in a preheated oven (180oºC) to bake for 60-70 minutes. When the bread items are done, remove them from the oven and let them cool down.

CHRISTMAS BREAD
6 loaves

This kind of bread has been a most important offering made during the Christmas period. All the ingredients pooled for its making are of prime quality (fine wheat flour, olive oil, dried fruits, sesame, spices). In addition, the Christmas bread is decorated with items indicative of the divine power. It is round with a cross made from dough lying on top. Alternatively, the cross appears in the form of a stamp, pressed before the bread is baked. Smaller crosses are made from leaves, figs, raisins, almonds, dried fruits shells, etc. Dried fruits symbolize the horn of plenty and fertility.

INGREDIENTS
2 kg white flour
30gr yeast
1 1/2 cups olive oil
3 cups sugar
1 teaspoon cinnamon
1 1/2 teaspoons clover, powdered
1 teaspoon mahleb, powdered
1 teaspoon aniseed
1 teaspoon coriander
2 vanilla shots
2 pieces mastic, crashed
1 teaspoon baking powder
1 cup orange juice
1/2 teaspoon salt

DIRECTIONS
1. Use a bowl to dissolve the yeast in two cups of lukewarm water. Add half the flour quantity and 3 tablespoons olive oil. Use your hands to mix everything in the bowl, until the flour absorbs all liquids and turns into thin dough. Cover the bowl with two pieces of cotton cloth and let it stand to rise in volume (2 hours).
2. In the meanwhile boil the coriander and aniseed in 1 1/2 cups of water; collect the drain and led it cool down.
3. When the dough has doubled in volume, add the sugar, salt, spices, rest of olive oil, the drained juice (coriander, aniseed), the orange juice and the remaining flour (previously mixed with the baking powder).
4. Knead the new mixture with your hands in fast motions (alternatively use a mixer at medium speed).

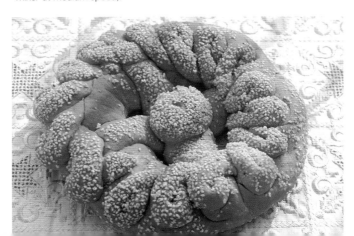

BREAD WITH ANISEED AND MAHLEB
(Bread from Sfakia)
4 loaves

The spices used in bread-making in Crete are but few, thus allowing bread a "clean" taste. The following recipe is an exception to the rule, as it involves more spices than customarily used. This bread is offered to guests during wedding celebrations, but it also makes delectable rusks (small, hard pieces of bread). The taste of aniseed and coriander is prominent.

INGREDIENTS

1 cup olive oil
1 kg white, soft flour
1/2 kg hard flour
25gr fresh yeast
1 tablespoon star aniseed
1/2 tablespoon cinnamon, grated
1/2 tablespoon mahleb, grated
1 teaspoon coriander
5 cloves, grated
1 cinnamon stick
3 pcs mastic, crashed
1 teaspoon salt
2 cups sugar
1 cup orange juice, fresh
3 tablespoons sesame

DIRECTIONS

1. Boil the coriander and cinnamon stick in a cup of water for 5-6 minutes and keep the drain (juice).

2. Use a large bowl to dissolve the yeast in a little lukewarm water. Add a few drops of olive oil and a little flour to make a thin paste. Cover the bowl with cotton cloth to keep warm, until the thin dough bubbles and rises.

3. When this dough is ready, add the olive oil, orange juice, the juice above (coriander, cinnamon stick), the rest of spices, salt and sugar. Mix them well with your hands to make a homogenous mixture.

4. Now, start adding flour in installments and at the same time knead the mixture. Add a little lukewarm water or additional flour, if necessary. The idea is to make homogenous, soft dough. Transfer the dough into a different, floured bowl. Cover the latter bowl with cotton cloth and put it in a warm place in the kitchen to let the dough rise (20-30 min.).

5. When the dough has almost doubled in volume, transfer it on a floured (preferably wooden) surface and knead again for 5-7 minutes. Divide the dough into pieces, depending on the size of the final product (bread / rolls) you require. When done, place the shaped items on a floured surface, cover with cotton cloth and let them rise.

6. Subsequently, transfer them in (a) greased baking sheet(s), brush them with sugar solution and sprinkle with sesame.

7. Preheat oven at 100°C; insert the baking sheets and raise temperature to 180°C. Bake for 45 minutes approximately.

8. When the loaves/rolls are done, let them cool down before cutting them to slices.

BARLEY RUSKS / HARD BREAD
(Cretan style)

As it can be preserved for long periods of time, this type of hard bread / rusks has been the staple of the poor, soldiers and seamen in antiquity. You can find it/them in the islands of Greece, e.g. in Santorini, Kimolos, Kassos, and Melos, as did the old travelers to Greece who, accustomed to "delicate" white French bread, scorned the bread/rusks on account of their dark appearance and hard texture. However, these bread items are tasty and wholesome. They absorb the aroma of the olive oil (see the Dakos recipe) and are one of the most favourite snacks in Crete.

INGREDIENTS

1 cup virgin olive oil

1 kg barley flour, incl. the bran

1/2 kg white flour

30gr fresh yeast

1 tablespoon salt

3 tablespoons red wine

DIRECTIONS

1. Use a bowl to dissolve the yeast in a little lukewarm water and stir in half the quantity of the white flour and let the mixture stand to double in volume (rise).

2. Place the wheat barley in another bowl and make a well in the middle to add in the salt, olive oil, wine and dissolved yeast mixture. Start kneading the mixture, alternating the addition of lukewarm water and a little from the white flour. Initially, this dough will be "heavy" and sticky. However, as you keep kneading and adding white flour, it will become more pliable and not stick to the sides of the bowl.

3. Cover the dough with two pieces of cotton cloth plus a small blanket, to keep it warm. Let the dough rise for 60-70 minutes.

4. Transfer the dough onto a lightly floured surface and knead it again for 6–7 minutes to make small, soft rolls (larger than a doughnut, without the hole in the middle). Use a sharp knife to deeply score the rolls horizontally and lightly score on the top and back a few times. Place dough rolls on a greased baking sheet and cover with a cotton towel. Let them rise for 50-60 minutes and bake them at 180ºC for 60 minutes.

5. Remove the baking sheets with the baked rolls/rusks from the oven and let them stand to cool down. Then cut them in half horizontally using a sharp knife. Place them back into the baking sheet and into the oven to bake at 50-70ºC for 5-7 hours. Keep the rusks at a dry and cool place.

Pastries

Pastry-making in the old days, from antiquity and thenceforth, involved the following prime materials: honey, cheese, milk, fruits (e.g. wild figs and pears, pomegranates, quinces, almonds, nuts, seeds (sesame, poppy, linseed) and flour (wheat, barley). Some of the above were used in ancient Greece to make a kind of pie known as plakounta. If honey was included, the pie was referred to as melitountas. Add sesame and linseed to the same and you have the sesame honey-sticks (itria). The list of pastries made in ancient Greece includes a variety of cheese pies made from fresh milk — milk-pies and pancakes.

GASTRIN, AN ANCIENT CRETAN DESERT

The islands of Kos, Samos (famous for its plakounta), and Paros were renowned in antiquity for their delicious pies. The island of Crete was also known for its famous glykinas and gastrin: "It is said that the Cretans make a small type of plakounta, the gastrin. They make it as follows: Nuts from the isle of Thassos and from Pontos, plus almonds and poppy flowers. Roast them with care, then place them in a clean mortar and crash them with double care. Mix all the fruits and pour the honey (dissolved in warm water) over them. Sprinkle them with a lot of pepper and knead them with your hands. The dark colour of the mixture is the result of the poppy flowers. Roll out the mixture on a surface and make a square of it. Sprinkle white sesame on top and pour boiled honey over it ..." (Athenaeus quoting Chrysippus of Tyana).

Many contemporary culinary experts from Greece associate gastrin with modern baklava. In a list of recipes issued in Alexandria (Egypt) in 1939 the gastrin is defined as a thick 'sesame pie', or a 'cake' compact with dried fruits (Andrew Dalby, linguist-historian).

The Byzantines were avid consumers of pastries and sweet wines. However, their favourite deserts were pancakes, sesame honey sticks pastelle (pasteli), as well as all kinds of pies stuffed with fresh cheese

(others topped with honey from Mt. Hymettus) and must-pies. The same is true of the ancient Greeks and Romans.

MODERN CRETAN PASTRIES

Milk, soft sour & sweet cheeses (e.g. sour/sweet myzithra, cream milk, milk-cheese, etc.) are the basis for a lot of pastries made in Crete. The combination of cheese, milk and dough yields a wide range of pastries, e.g. custard pies (galaktoboureko), Easter kalitsounia, Boureki (pie/pastry), Bougatsa (milk/cheese pie), and a variety of cheese pies (myzithra being the main ingredient). A lot of the above are in the form of little cheese pies whose taste ranges from sweet and piquant.

Another category, equally significant, is that involving flour, semolina, dried/fresh fruits and butter/olive oil. This category yields halva, baklava, ravani, and a range of oven pies (ladopita, grape-juice pies, fanouropita, raisin-pies, yogurt pies, dried-fruit pies, kourabies, and melomakarouno).

A sub-category of the above includes pastries with dough as their predominant or only ingredient. This yields such crunchy pastries as xerotigana, tiganopites, loukoumata or kourkoubinoi.

All kinds of rolls and rusks come under a special category of pastries for daily use. They are very common and used as stand-alone snacks, coffee/tea dips or offered as a treat to guests.

FANOUROPITA
Serves 10-15

INGREDIENTS

1 cup olive oil

1 cup the juice from boiled cinnamon sticks

1 cup sugar

5-6 cloves, crashed

1 teaspoon soda

1 teaspoon baking powder

1 cup almonds, coarsely crashed

2 tablespoons brandy

1 kg flour, all purpose

DIRECTIONS

1. Pour the olive oil and sugar into a large bowl and mix them with your hands for 3-4 minutes.

2. Gradually stir in by hand the cinnamon juice, cloves, soda (dissolved in the brandy), almonds, flour and baking powder. Mix well for 5 more minutes.

3. Pour the mixture into a baking pan (No 35), insert it into a preheated oven and bake at 180°C for 70 minutes.

WALNUT PIE
Serves 10-15

INGREDIENTS

10 eggs (whites only)

10 tablespoons sugar

10 tablespoons semolina, fine

2 tablespoons cinnamon, powder

1 tablespoon cloves, grated

1 tablespoon baking powder

2 cups walnuts, coarsely chopped

Syrup:

2 glasses sugar

3 glasses water

DIRECTIONS

1. Whisk the egg-whites to a not too tight meringue. Add the sugar in tablespoon installments and the semolina, stirring at the same time. Add the cinnamon, cloves, baking powder and the nuts. Slowly stir the mixture using a wooden ladle.

2. Pour the mixture into a baking pan (No 30) and bake at 180°C for 50 minutes approximately.

3. Prepare the syrup and boil it for 10 minutes. When the pie is done, let it stand to cool down and then pour the syrup over it.

VASILOPITA WITH SYRUP

Serves 10

INGREDIENTS

2 cups sugar

1 cup fresh butter

2 tablespoons olive oil

3 eggs

1 tablespoon orange rind, grated

1 teaspoon lemon rind, grated

1 cup orange juice

1 tablespoon baking powder

1 tablespoon brandy

2 tablespoons almonds, coarsely crashed

4-5 cups soft flour

Syrup:

1 cup orange juice

3 tablespoons sugar

DIRECTIONS

1. Place the butter and sugar in a mixer bowl and run the mixer for 2-3 minutes. Add in the eggs, orange and lemon rind, brandy, olive oil, orange juice and flour (previously mixed with the baking powder). Run the mixer for 2-3 minutes; add the almonds and run the mixer again for 2 minutes.

2. Pour the mixture in a greased baking pan and bake at 180ºC for 45-50 minutes. To check if the pie is done, insert the blade of a knife in the center of the pie. When the knife comes out "clean", the pie is done.

3. To make the syrup: boil the orange juice with the sugar for 7 minutes. As soon as you remove the pie from the oven, pour the syrup over it.

ALMOND PIE
WITH ORANGE CREAM
Serves 10-15

INGREDIENTS

320gr almonds, powdered

300gr fine sugar (powder)

7 eggs

(separate yolks from whites)

2 oranges

(boiled and later ground)

4 tablespoons semolina

2 teaspoons baking powder

3 tablespoons butter

Syrup:

2 cups water

2 cups sugar

Cream:

5 glasses milk

6 tablespoons corn flour

8 tablespoons sugar

lemon rind

2 eggs, whisked

1 cup roasted almonds

DIRECTIONS

1. Wire-whisk the egg whites in a metallic bowl to get a soft meringue. Use a second bowl to beat the butter with the sugar to get a thin "white" paste. In the same bowl add the mashed oranges, semolina, egg yolks and almonds. Beat the mixture to get homogenous paste.

2. Use a wooden spatula to mix in the meringue in the second mixture. Empty this mixture into a lightly greased baking dish; spread it evenly and bake at 180°C for 45-50 minutes. In the meanwhile prepare the syrup, the fluidity of which must resemble that of olive oil.

3. As soon as the pie in the baking dish is done, pour the syrup (at room temperature) over it. Prepare the cream as follows: bring four glasses of milk to the boil; add the sugar, lemon rind and stir to dissolve the sugar. Stir in the corn flour, which you have previously dissolved in a glass of milk (from the portion of milk reserved). Stir the mixture slowly using a spatula, until the mixture starts to coagulate. Take the cream off the ring and remove the lemon rind. Allow the cream to cool down for 7-9 minutes. Stir in the whisked eggs and pour the cream over the pie. Spread evenly using a spatula and sprinkle with roasted almonds.

RAISINS PIE
Serves 10-15

INGREDIENTS

1 kg flour

1 cup olive oil

600gr sugar

1 1/2 cups lukewarm water

2 teaspoons soda

2 tablespoons brandy

the juice from 2 oranges

1 teaspoon nutmeg

1 teaspoon cinnamon, powder

6-7 cloves, crashed

3 cups raisins, halved

DIRECTIONS

1. Whisk the olive oil and sugar in a bowl for 5 minutes.

2. Add the brandy, spices, soda, orange juice, raisins and, lastly, the flour. Stir the ingredients using your hand, to mix all into a thick paste

3. Empty the mixture into a greased baking pan, No. 36, and bake at 180°C for 45 minutes.

BAKLAVA
WITH ALMONDS AND NUTS
Serves 6-10

INGREDIENTS

1 packet phyllo sheets

3 cups almonds and nuts
(equal portions), coarsely
crashed

3 tablespoons sugar

1 teaspoon cinnamon

1 small nugget of mastic
(crashed with a 1 tbsp sugar)

10-15 cloves

1 cup fresh butter

Syrup:

2 cups sugar

1 cup water

1 cinnamon stick

DIRECTIONS

1. Use a bowl to mix the sugar with the coarsely crashed almonds, nuts, cinnamon and mastic. This is your filling.

2. Use a shallow and rectangular baking pan (preferably 9x12x2) and grease the bottom and sides with melted butter. Lay in 5-6 phyllo sheets, brushing each on top. The phyllo layers may run a little over the sides of the baking pan; fold the sides in or cut them out.

3. Pour in and uniformly spread the filling over the top phyllo layer. Sprinkle with a little melted butter. Cover the filling with an equal number of phyllo sheets from the packet, brushing each with butter on top. Use a sharp knife to score across the completed baklava into triangles or diamonds. Stick a clove on each scored shape.

4. Insert the baklava into the oven and bake at 180°C for 50-55 minutes. In the meantime, prepare the syrup and let it cool down. As soon as the baklava is done, remove it from the oven and brush the top with a little butter and then pour the syrup on top. Let the syrup sip in the baklava and then cut to pre-scored servings.

ALMOND PIE
Serves 10-15

INGREDIENTS

1 1/2 cups almonds, finely
chopped

7 whole eggs

1 tablespoon breadcrumbs

1 teaspoon cloves, grated

1 teaspoon cinnamon, grated

1 teaspoon baking powder

1 glass sugar

1/2 kg white flour

Syrup:

2 cups sugar

1 cup water

1 tablespoon orange rind,
grated

DIRECTIONS

1. Wire-whisk the eggs in a deep bowl. Add the breadcrumbs, cloves, cinnamon and sugar. Mix the baking power with the flour and add the mixture into the bowl. Finally, add the almonds and work the mixture with your hands for 2-3 minutes (correct with a little flour if the mixture is too runny).

2. Place the mixture into a baking pan (No 30) and insert it into the oven to bake at 180°C for 55 minutes.

3. Prepare the syrup and boil it for 6-7 minutes. When the pie is done, remove it from the oven; let it stand to cool down; cut it to individual servings and pour the warm syrup over it.

HALVA

Serves 10

INGREDIENTS

4 glasses water

2 1/2 glasses sugar

1/2 lemon, the juice squeezed out

2-3 cinnamon sticks

1 glass olive oil

2 glasses coarse semolina

2 tablespoons cinnamon, grated

100 gr almonds, roasted and chopped

DIRECTIONS:

1. Pour the water in a pot; add the sugar, squeezed-out half lemon and the cinnamon sticks. Boil for 10 min. approximately and strain (keep). This is your syrup.

2. Pick another pot to add the olive oil and when it starts to steam add the semolina and stir continuously, otherwise the semolina will burn. As soon as the semolina is done it takes a golden (yellowish) colour. Add in the syrup (hot, careful!) and lower heat.

3. Add 1 tablespoon of cinnamon and let the halva on the heat for 5 more minutes. Remove the pot from heat and cover with a towel. Sprinkle a cake tin with a little cinnamon, pour in the halva and spread evenly. Sprinkle the rest of the cinnamon and turn the cake tin over on a large dish. Top with the chopped almonds.

GALAKTOBOUREKO
(Custard Pie)
Serves 8-10

INGREDIENTS

1/4 cup semolina, fine

1 1/2 cups sugar

1/2 cup corn flour

6 eggs, lightly whisked

1 lt milk

1/2 cup semolina (additional)

12 phyllo sheets

130gr fresh butter

1 teaspoon lemon rind, grated
(optional)

Syrup:

1 teaspoon lemon juice

1 1/2 cups sugar

3/4 cup water

1 cinnamon stick

DIRECTIONS:

1. In a bowl mix well the 1/4 cup semolina, sugar, corn flour, eggs, and rind.

2. Bring the milk to the boil and gradually pour it in the hot mixture above, whisking at the same time.

3. Transfer the mixture into a pot and stir while heating it. Gradually add the remaining semolina and stir. Do not let the mixture come to the boil. Remove the mixture from the heat and set it aside to cool down. This is your custard.

4. Grease a fireproof pan (22x30cm) and place a phyllo sheet at the bottom, making sure that it comes up the pan sides. Brush the phyllo sheet with butter and place five more phyllos on top of each other brushing them very well with butter in between.

5. Pour in the custard on the phyllo stack and spread it uniformly with a spatula. Lay in the remaining phyllo sheets, brushing them in between. Cut out or fold in the protruding phyllo sheet sides.

6. Brush the top layer with a little butter and score across into triangle or diamond shapes. Bake on the center rack at 180ºC for 45 minutes. Prepare the syrup, not too thick, and let it cool down completely.

7. When you remove the galaktoboureko hot from the oven, brush its surface with a little butter and pour the syrup over.

8. Cool thoroughly before cutting and serving. Store in the refrigerator.

ZOURNADAKIA

30-40 servings

INGREDIENTS

1/2 kg walnuts, coarsely crashed

1/2 kg almonds, coarsely crashed

1 cup sesame

1/2 cup sugar

1 tablespoon cinnamon

1 cup olive oil

1 packet phyllo sheets

Syrup:

2 cups sugar

1 1/2 cups water

1 teaspoon lemon juice

DIRECTIONS

1. In a bowl mix the sugar, walnuts, almonds, sesame and cinnamon. This is your "filling".

2. Cut out phyllo strips approximately 3-4 cm wide. Brush the top of strips with a little olive oil and sprinkle them with a small quantity from the filling (not entire length of strip, but a little short from both ends).

3. Start rolling in the strips tight from end to end. Repeat the same with all of the strips until you have exhausted the filling.

4. Place the rolled items (zournadakia) in a lightly greased pan and bake in moderate oven for 25-30 minutes until the zournadakia are golden brown.

5. When done, remove them from the oven and let them cool down completely. In the meantime, make the syrup. While the syrup is hot, use a perforated spoon to pick up four zournadakia which you dip in the syrup for a few minutes. Remove them from the syrup with the same spoon (let syrup drain) and place them in a large dish. Repeat until you have dipped all zournadakia. Serve them at room temperature.

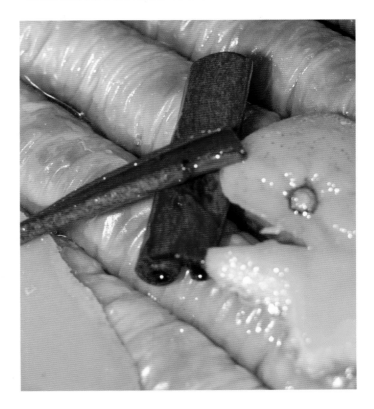

XEROTIGANA

35-40 pieces

INGREDIENTS

1 kg hard flour

2 tablespoons raki / tsipouro /grap

2 tablespoons olive oil

1 teaspoon salt

2-3 cups water

3-4 cups corn oil / sunflower oil

Syrup:

1 kg sugar

1 cup honey

1/2 lt water

1 cinnamon stick

1 cup walnuts, finely grated

1 tablespoon sesame

DIRECTIONS

1. Pour the flour in a large blender bowl and make a well in the middle. Add in the raki / tsipouro / grap, olive oil, salt and water. Run the blender at medium speed for 10 minutes to get homogenous and rather tight dough. Cover the bowl with cotton cloth and let the dough rest for 10 minutes.

2. Divide the dough in two equal pieces (the size of a peach) to roll out two phyllo sheets, 1 cm thick and 15 cm long. Using one sheet, cut along a phyllo strip 2-3 cm wide and make a fairly loose spiral out of it, carefully manipulating the inside coils so that the item looks like a large rose (true, it takes some imagination, but you can skip the rose intricacies). Repeat the cutting of strips and shaping the same into coils / 'roses'. Repeat the process with the remaining strips and phyllo sheets.

3. Fry the coils/'roses' into scorching oil for 3-4 minutes, until golden brown on both sides.

4. Use a perforated spatula to remove the xerotigana and place them on a large dish lined with kitchen paper.

5. Syrup: Mix the sugar, honey, water and cinnamon and boil them for 10-13 minutes. Dip each of the xerotigana into the hot syrup for 1-2 minutes; place them into a large dish and sprinkle them with grated walnuts and sesame.

LITTLE HARD DIPS WITH SESAME AND OLIVE OIL
30-40 pieces

INGREDIENTS

1 1/2 cups olive oil

1 1/2 cups sugar

1 cup orange juice

20gr baking powder

2 tablespoons black sesame

1 shot cumin

5-7 cups white flour, soft

DIRECTIONS

1. Pour the olive oil and sugar in a large bowl. Mix them using your hands. Fry the sesame for 3-4 minutes then add it to the bowl along with the orange juice and cumin.

2. Mix the flour with the baking powder and gradually add this mixture into the bowl and knead until you get pliable dough hard in consistency.

3. Use this dough to shape little loaves 16cm long, 3cm thick, 3 cm wide approximately and score them at 2cm distances. Place the loaves in a greased baking sheet and bake at 180ºC for 45-50 minutes.

4. When done, remove the baking sheet from the oven and cut the loaves through the score lines. Place the pieces back into the baking sheet and bake them at 60ºC for 2-3 hours to harden them more.

LITTLE CAKES WITH SESAME
30-40 pieces

INGREDIENTS

400-600gr all-purpose flour

1 1/2 glasses butter

1/2 glass olive oil

1 1/2 glasses sugar

1/2 glass warm water

1 teaspoon soda

1 small lemon, the juice

2 eggs (to brush)

200gr sesame

DIRECTIONS

1. Heat the butter with the olive oil and let the mixture cool down a little. Stir in the sugar to dissolve in the mixture.

2. Next, add the warm water, soda (dissolved in the lemon juice) and as much flour as it takes to get fluffy dough.

3. Pick approximately a tablespoon or more from the dough and roll it to 7-8 cm cylinders (thick in the middle and tapering off a little at both ends). Dip the cylinders in the whisked eggs and roll them over sesame. Shape cylinders to circles, with hole in the middle (approx. 1 little finger gap).

4. Place rolls on a baking sheet and bake them at 170ºC for 25 minutes.

PATOUDA FROM SITEIA – STUFFED BISCUITS

30-40 pieces

INGREDIENTS

250gr butter, unsalted

2 water-glasses olive oil

1 teaspoon soda

3 teaspoons baking powder

1 water-glass sugar

3/4 water-glass orange juice

1 1/2 kg flour (approx.)

Filling:

1/2 kg shelled walnuts and almonds

1 nutmeg, grated

1/2 teaspoon cinnamon

1/2 teaspoon cloves

1 1/2 tablespoons olive oil

breadcrumbs, 1-2 slices

2 tablespoons sugar

1 tablespoon honey

To sprinkle:

Orange blossom water

Sugar powder

DIRECTIONS

1. Mix and beat the butter and sugar in a bowl until you get a kind of 'white' paste. Then add the olive oil, orange juice and soda (previously dissolved in little orange juice). Mix the flour with the baking powder and gradually add this mixture into the former. Stir to mix well.

2. Knead well to get firm dough that does not stick to the sides of the bowl. Cover the bowl with a cotton cloth and let it rest for 30 minutes.

3. The filling: heat 1/4 glass of water to dissolve the sugar and honey. Pour this solution into a bowl, add the rest of the filling ingredients and stir well.

4. Use the dough to roll out a single phyllo (1-2 cm thick). Use a round cake tin (8 cm in diameter) and press it on the phyllo to cut out round dough discs. Place a tablespoon from the filling in the middle of a disc and fold to crescent shape. Secure the perimeter of the crescent by pressing on it the back (tine-side) of a fork. Repeat with the remaining dough discs and, presto, your patouda are ready to bake.

5. Place the patouda on a greased baking dish and insert them in a preheated oven to bake at 180ºC for 30 minutes approximately.

6. As soon as you take them out of the oven, sprinkle them with blossom water and sugar powder.

ALMOND BISCUITS

30-40 pieces

INGREDIENTS

1kg almonds, blanched

800gr sugar

8 eggs, the whites only

6 tablespoons brandy

DIRECTIONS

1. Heat the oven to 180oºC. Collect the almonds; set 20-30 whole almonds aside (the number should correspond to the number of cookies), chop and place the rest in a blender to turn them into powder.

2. Mix the sugar and powdered almonds in a bowl. Pick another bowl to whisk in the egg whites and as soon as they start to form bubbles, add in the sugar with the powdered almonds. Also, stir in the brandy.

3. Line a baking sheet with grease paper and brush it with butter. On a lightly floured surface, knead lightly and roll out to approximately 1cm thick. Shape biscuits by hand or cut into rounds with a 6 cm cutter. Re-roll and re-cut any trimmings. Stick a whole almond on each round. Bake at 180ºC for 20-25 min. Allow space between rounds to expand in the baking sheet.

4. Remove biscuits from the oven and let them cool down, then transfer them into a plate.

KOURABIEDES
(Almond biscuits with sugar powder)

30-40 pieces

INGREDIENTS

500gr butter (margarine)

400gr fresh butter

2 cups sugar

800gr shelled almonds

3 egg-yolks

1 egg-white

2 tablespoons brandy

3 vanillas

1 teaspoon cinnamon

1 teaspoon soda

1 tablespoon lemon juice

1kg flour, all purpose

3-4 cups sugar powder

DIRECTIONS

1. Place the butter, margarine, sugar, and brandy in a mixer bowl and run the mixer at medium speed. Shell and roast the almonds in a medium heat oven for 7-12 minutes. Remove the almonds and crush them (coarsely or finely).

2. Add the egg yolks into the mixer bowl and run the mixer again for 2-3 minutes.

3. Add the cinnamon, soda (dissolved in the lemon juice), almonds, and vanillas and run the mixer again. Whisk the egg-white to meringue and gradually add it to the mixture in the bowl. Transfer the mixture from the mixer bowl into another bowl and gradually add in the flour. Start kneading by hand to get firm dough, add as much flour as it takes.

4. Pick a little less than half a handful of dough, round and pat it to approximately 1 cm thick, or use the proper cookie cutter. Repeat the process until you have exhausted the dough. Place the rounds on a greased baking sheet and bake at 200ºC for 20-25 minutes.

5. When done, remove the kourabiedes from the oven, let them cool down completely and sprinkle them with sugar powder.

MELOMAKARONA
(Honey Biscuits)
30-40 pieces

INGREDIENTS

2 cups olive oil

1 cup sugar

2 teaspoons (level) baking powder

1 teaspoon soda

8 tablespoons orange juice, fresh

1/2 tablespoon cloves, pulverized

1/2 tablespoon cinnamon

7-8 cups flour

Syrup:

2 cups honey

2 cups sugar

2 cups water

3 tablespoons sesame, roasted

1 cup walnuts, crushed

DIRECTIONS

1. Whisk the sugar and the olive oil to get a thin, white paste. Add in the soda (dissolved in little orange juice), the baking powder, cloves, cinnamon and the flour.

2. Knead oblong (flat in the middle) sticks, 3-4 cm wide, 7-8 cm long and 1 1/2 - 2 cm thick (usually thicker in the middle and tapering off a little at the ends – more like an oval shape). Bake the sticks at 180ºC for 30 minutes approximately. When done, let them cool down.

3. Make the syrup and let it cool down. As soon as the melomakarona are done, remove them from the oven and soak each in the syrup for 3-4 minutes.

4. Place them in a large plate and sprinkle them with the mixture of sesame and crushed walnuts.

Kalitsounia
(From sweet cheese)

In many ancient Greek texts we can find references to "thin bread" preparations or dough with either a longitudinal, triangular or round shape. This "bread" or dough was usually stuffed with various soft cheeses, spices, dill, and mint and topped with honey and sesame. Cheese pies have been with us for many centuries. For example, Sophron of Syracuse (c. 430 BC) wrote about the "*tyroenta* bread", i.e. a kind of cheese pie. Centuries later the Cretans make use of the same raw materials to produce delicious pies from fresh, full fat milk taken in the months of April and May (e.g. *myzithra*, cream milk [*anthotyros*], *tyromalama*, and sour *myzithra* [from the whey of *feta* and *kefalotyri* cheese and from sheep's and cow's milk]. The cheese is folded in thin, crunchy pies and served at Easter. These pies are usually prepared on Easter Thursday or early on Easter Saturday. The ingredients include mint, mastic, orange rind, cinnamon, even lemon leaves or honey. Their popular name is *kalitsounia*, usually round or triangular in shape, but also square.

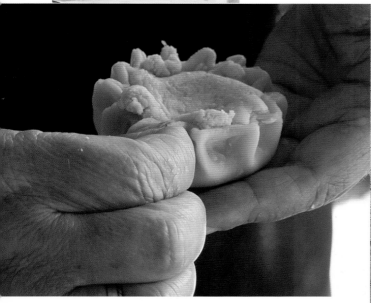

KALITSOUNIA OF SITEIA

40 pieces approximately

INGREDIENTS

1 1/2 kg flour

1 cup olive oil

1 cup sugar

2 eggs

150gr yogurt

1 shot vanilla

1/2 teaspoon mastic

15 lemon leaves

1 cup white sesame

2 tablespoons fresh yeast

Filling:

1kg *myzithra* cheese

1 egg

2 tablespoons sugar

4 tablespoons honey

1 teaspoon cinnamon (powder)

DIRECTIONS

1. In a bowl dissolve the yeast in 1 1/2 cups lukewarm water. Gradually add half the quantity of flour and knead to get soft dough that does not stick to your hands. Cover the dough with a cotton cloth and put the bowl in a warm place to rise in the next 3-4 hours.

2. Use another bowl to add the sugar, olive oil, eggs and yogurt and mix them with your hands. Add in the dough from the first bowl and 1 cup of lukewarm water.

3. Use yet another bowl (small) to mix the vanillas with the mastic (powdered). Add this mixture into the previous bowl and knead very well to get fluffy and soft dough that does not stick to your hands. Cover the dough with a cotton cloth and let it stand to double in volume (2 hours approx.).

4. Prepare the filling by mixing the *myzithra*, sugar, honey, whisked egg and cinnamon.

5. Divide the dough in small pieces and roll a thin (approx. 1 cm) phyllo. Use a saucer (5cm diam.) to cut out dough discs. The dough should be enough for approximately 40 such discs. Pick a dough disc and place a tablespoon of filling in the middle; spread out a little and fold in the perimeter to almost cover the filling.

6. When you have exhausted to dough and/or the filling, let the kalitsounia aside to rise (1 hour). Then brush them with whisked egg and sprinkle with sesame.

7. Line a baking tin with grease paper and cook the *kalitsounia* in a preheated oven at 180ºC until golden brown on top (approx. 30 minutes).

8. Serve them in a platter with lemon leaves wedged among them.

KALITSOUNIA WITH MINT

INGREDIENTS

640gr butter

1kg sugar

10gr ammonia

6 eggs

3 cups milk

1 shot vanilla

600-800 gr flour, or as much as it takes

Filling:

1kg *myzithra*

1 egg

3 tablespoons sugar

4-5 fresh mint leaves

DIRECTIONS

1. Use a bowl to mix the butter and sugar. Dissolve the ammonia in the milk and add this into the bowl, as well as the eggs (whisked), the vanilla and flour. Knead using your hands to get fluffy dough.

2. Let the dough rest and prepare the filling: use a bowl to add the myzithra, sugar, egg and mint. Mix all well using your hands.

3. Pick a handful of dough to roll it out into a large phyllo 1/2 cm thick. Cut out discs 4-5 cm in diameter. Cut out as many discs as your dough allows.

4. Place a tablespoon of filling in the center of the dough disc; raise the perimeter of the disc and pinch it around using your thumb and index finger. Actually, you raise, pinch and press a little forward and down.

5. Place the *kalitsounia* in baking sheets and brush them with a little butter and whisked egg. Bake at 180ºC for 30-40 minutes.

KALITSOUNIA IN TART MOULDS
20 pieces approximately

INGREDIENTS

100gr milk butter

150gr Corfu butter

160gr sugar

2 eggs

4 cups soft flour

Filling:

1kg sweet *myzithra*

1 egg

4 cups sugar

cinnamon

Tart moulds: round, 3-5 cm in diameter

DIRECTIONS

1. In a bowl (or mixer) mix the butter with the sugar to get a smooth paste. Add the eggs and the flour in installments while you knead at the same time. Continue kneading a little more until you get a homogenous mixture.

2. Use another bowl to make the filling: add in the myzithra, egg and sugar and mix them well.

3. Line the tart moulds with the dough and fill them with the filling.

4. Brush the top of the kalitsounia with whisked egg and sprinkle them with cinnamon. Insert the filled tart moulds in a preheated oven (180ºC) and bake for 25 minutes.

5. When done, remove the moulds and allow them to cool down before you remove the kalitsounia (use a little sharp knife the tip of which you run perimetrically between the mould and the edge of the kalitsounia).

SPOON DESSERTS

FIGS WITH HONEY AND SPICES

INGREDIENTS

10-15 dried figs

1 cinnamon (small bark)

3 cloves

1 laurel leaf

1 tsp honey

1 cup almonds, blanched

1 cup thyme (tea)

DIRECTIONS

1. Empty the thyme tea in a saucepan, add the laurel leaf, figs, cinnamon, cloves and honey. Add two cups of water and simmer for 6-8 minutes.

2. Cover the saucepan with its lid and continue simmering until the figs get tender and soak well in the spiced juice.

3. Serve them with their syrup and almonds.

BIGARADE IN ORANGE JUICE
45 pieces

INGREDIENTS
10-12 bigarades, approximately

1 kg sugar

4 cups orange juice

DIRECTIONS
1. Wash the bigarades well and let them drain or pat them dry. Grate them on a fine grater to remove the bitter part of their skin.

2. Score the bigarades cross-wise from top to bottom (along 4 meridians) and carefully remove the peels, making sure not to tear them. The peels are almost rectangular, tapering a little at both ends.

3. Roll in the peels tight and secure them using a toothpick or string.

4. Boil the peels in fresh water twice, 5 minutes each time and always dispose of the water. Place the boiled peels in a bowl with cold water. Keep them there for two days and change the water each morning and evening. This will turn them sweeter. The longer you let them in the water, the sweeter they become.

5. Strain and place the bigarade peels on absorbent paper. Remove the toothpick or string, squeeze them to drain well and place them in a pot.

6. Let them stand in the pot for 5-6 hours and then add in the sugar and orange juice. Boil the dessert until the syrup is done. Remove pot from heat and let the dessert stand for 24 hours in the pot. Boil again the following day for 10 minutes, for the water in the pot to evaporate.

7. Let the dessert cool down and place it in jars.

APPLE
(codlin: very small variety of apples)

INGREDIENTS
20 codlins, green

800gr sugar

1 1/2 cups water

30 almonds, blanched

20 cloves

2 lemons

DIRECTIONS
1. Wash, peel and core the codlins and place them in a bowl of water and lemon juice (1 lemon).

2. Boil the sugar in the water (1 1/2 cups) for 5-7 minutes, then add the codlins to simmer until the syrup takes a pale caramel color.

3. Remove codlins using a perforated spoon and place them in a large bowl to drain. Stuff the codlins with an almond and a clove.

4. Place the codlins in large glass jars and fill in with syrup.

QUINCE
(2 medium-sized glass jars)

INGREDIENTS

1 kg quinces

1 kg sugar

3 glasses water

1 lemon, the juice

2 sprigs pelargonium

DIRECTIONS

1. Wash, peel and grate the quinces a little.

2. Use a large pot to boil the water and sugar for 10 minutes, then add the quinces.

3. Boil the quinces until you are satisfied with the constitution of the syrup, then add the pelargonium and the lemon juice.

GRAPES
2 jars

INGREDIENTS

1 kg grapes, no pits

700gr sugar

1 cup water

1 pelargonium leaf

1 teaspoon lemon juice

DIRECTIONS

1. Pick the firm and juicy grapes and rinse them well under tap water. Spread grapes on a cotton cloth to drain.

2. Boil the sugar in water over low heat and stir to dissolve well. When you are satisfied with the constitution of the syrup, add in the grapes, raise heat and skim out froth. Add the lemon juice and pelargonium. Boil the dessert for 5-6 minutes. As soon as done, transfer the dessert into clean glass jars and seal tight. Keep jars at a cool place or in the fridge.

Raki

In the month of November the new wine crop is on its way to maturity. The new wines are translucent, charming, assertive and "fidgety". This is time for "moon shining" *raki*, the local drink of Crete. In spite of the fact that raki is made from the residues (or "shreds') of grapes, it is a strong, full-bodied drink, very much like the temperament of the Cretans.

This is the season that scores of "cauldrons" (make-shift distilleries) are in full operation, day and night, patiently dripping away the precious, crystal clear drink of the Cretans.

An invitation to attend this "moon shining" process during a rainy evening in November is considered a great honour for the Cretans. This invitation comes with the knowledge that participants will enjoy not only the intoxicating and aromatic drink dripping from the "cauldron", but they will also savour the "*mezethes*" (delicious snacks) (e.g. meat and potatoes on charcoal), not to mention the performance by local musicians.

RAKI PRODUCTION PROCESS

Following the "dancing on the grapes" or the mechanical crushing of the same and the collection of the must, what remains are the residues of the crushed grapes, i.e. their skin, pits, etc. These must residues are stored in large clay jars or barrels for 30 days, to ferment. Subsequently, this "precious" load is transferred to an open-air distillery where the residues are placed in a cauldron and heated over a strong fire fed with logs. While the must residues are boiling, fumes build up in the large cauldron and travel through attached coils where they are cooled and liquefied into a translucent liquid, the raki.

This drink is twice or three times as strong as the average wine. Actually, the stronger portion of raki comes out during the first 10 to 15 minutes of distillation.

RAKI IN THE KITCHEN

Being quite a strong alcoholic drink, it is always accompanied with tasty mezethes (snacks), i.e. raisins, dried fruit, fresh butter beans, olives, baked potatoes, pork sausages, snails or even urchin salad!! I suggest that you store a bottle of raki in your kitchen; you will find it handy. You may not drink much, but surely you could add raki to your meals while cooking.

Experimenting with all sorts of ingredients, the women of Crete discovered that raki to dough adds an exciting flavour to pastries and desserts. For example, raki renders the Cretan spinach or herb pies, *sarikopites* and *myzithra* pies, crunchy and delicious.

Raki scented with lemon leaves, fennel or mastic is ideal for marinading pork chops or apaki (smoked pork). Also, raki is used to make the "tipsy cookies" in the town of Neapolis in the prefecture of Lassithi.

LIQUEUR FROM RAKI

Cretan women are quite imaginative when it comes to
house-keeping, including cooking. And although they
definitely drink raki much less than their husbands, they
do know how to 'tame' this "rogue" drink that
invigorates body and soul.

By adding fruit, e.g. various cherry varieties and
pomegranate seeds, the Cretan women gave raki a
reddish hue and sweet taste. Other substances added
to raki are: honey, grape syrup, cinnamon and cloves.
In western Crete they add thyme sprigs and lavender
leaves. When warm this drink can treat cold in winter.
My grandmother did something simpler: she would put
a few orange or mandarin peels in a jar, sprinkled them
with a little sugar, add cloves and top the jars with raki.
Subsequently, she would bask these jars under the hot
Cretan sun in the month of spring.

WINE

According to Cretan mythology, it was Cronus, the father
of Zeus that brought the vine to the island and taught
Cretans the art of viticulture. This is to show that
viticulture is not only an ancient tradition, but a very
important activity in Crete.

Numerous prehistoric finds lend incontestable support
to the claim that Crete produced excellent qualities of
wine in such amounts as to make this product good for
exports around the Mediterranean basin.

Thanks to Michael Ventris (1922-1956), the English
architect and classical scholar who deciphered the
Linear B Tablets of Knossos, we now know that wine
was popular in Minoan Crete. The Tablets make
quantitative references to wine produced locally. An
inscription on the same Tablets reads as follows: "... a
precious gift [the wine], patroned by the son of Zeus

and Semeli, king Minos himself; the Cretan wine was made in compliance with the recipe which, according to tradition, was given to the king by Apollo..."

Ancient wine presses were found scattered around the island of Crete – a testimony to a proliferating viticulture and grape varieties. In the sites of Vathypetro and Archanes archaeologists discovered the oldest wine presses in the island, while the Fourni location can boast of the most elaborate ancient wine press. Other locations where wine presses were found are: Zakros, Knossos, Phaestos, Myrtos, Malia and Gournia. All locations with ancient wine presses also featured pottery workshops for the production of ornate clay jars (amphorae) where the Minoans stored the wine.

Roman women were not allowed to drink wine from grapes, excluding the Passo, i.e. a type of Cretan wine made from the crushing of raisins. The Passo was sweet and good for quenching thirst.

A gold ring of the Middle-Minoan period (ca 1600 BC) represents in relief four bare-breasted Minoan women dancing with hands raised and holding sacred objects. One of them holds a crater (large cup) and sips wine, while the other three hold bunches of grapes.

Ancient physicians recommended the Cretan wine in the cure of numerous diseases as they believed that the local wine imparts strength and longevity.

An inscription on the Levina column (Ledas area) says that Publius Granius Rufus, the Roman governor of the area, suffered from acute pain and was cured by the local wine: "... God sent for me to give me a remedy of barley flour and old wine...". Another remedy on the same column reads: "... [he/she] took pepper with wine and found health ..."

VITICULTURE AND WINE PRODUCTION IN CRETE

Crete is one of the few areas in the world where one can find very old vineyards producing grape varieties that make excellent wine. Cretan vineyards benefit from the mild climate prevailing in this part of the world and from the mountainous relief of the island, i.e. long sunny days, cool winds from the north and high rising mountains protecting the crops from hot, south winds occasionally sweeping across the Libyan Sea.

Currently, a total area of approximately 9 hectares is available for cultivation of wine grapes in Crete. Approximately 4 hectares are located in the prefecture of Heraklion (corresponding to 1,5 hect. for VQRPD wines and 2,5 hect. for common wines), 2,4 hectares in Hania, 1,4 hect. in Rethymnon and 1,2 hect. in Lassithi.

Viticulture Areas in Crete

Wine grapes are cultivated from one end of the island to the other, but the most significant areas are located in the north of the island, where you will find the oldest European vineyards comprising a wide range of self-rooting vine varieties. On the island of Crete there are four areas (corresponding to the 4 prefectures) producing Appellation of Origin wines.

Prefecture of Heraklion
It is the largest among the prefectures and most prolific in terms of quantity and quality of wines. This prefecture hosts three of the four areas producing Appellation of Origin wines: Peza, Archanes and Dafnes.

• Peza area
This wine area comprises the vineyards of the neighbouring 15 villages in the Pediada province. The most important of these villages are: Peza, Kounavoi, Ayies Paraskies and Houdetsi. The area produces two types of wines: Peza Red and Peza White wines.

The former, Peza Red, combines the grape varieties of Kotsifali (80%) and Mantilari (20%). The sugar content of this wine must not be in excess of 188gr per liter and the yield of the vineyards in grapes per one thousand square meters must not be in excess of 1000 kg. This wine is best matured in oak barrels for at least one year.
The Peza White wine is produced from the Velana grape variety. Its content in alcohol usually ranges from 11.0 to 12.5 vol, while the yield of these vineyards per one thousand square meters should not exceed 1,200 kg of wine grapes.

• Archanes Area
This area hosts the vineyards of six neighbouring villages: Archanes, Kato Archanes, Skalani, Vasilies, Profitis Elias and Ayios Sylas. The area produces the Archanes Red wine, which combines the grape varieties of Kotsifali (80%) Mantilari (20%).

• Dafnes Area
This area hosts the vineyards of twenty villages. The most important of these villages are: Ayia Varvara, Gergeri, Ayios Myronas, Avgeniki, Ano & Kato Assites. The area produces the Dafnes Red wine.
This wine is produced from the Liatiko variety and the types of red wine produced range from dry to sweet. The sugar content ranges from 188gr/lt for the dry type, 221gr/lt for the sweet and 238gr/lt for the naturally sweet type. The yield of vineyards should not exceed 800kg of grapes per 1,000m2.

Prefecture of Hania
This is the second in size and viticulture significance prefecture of Crete. It features the Romaiko grape variety, dominant in the area of Sfakia, and the Liatiko variety. Wine production is more of a home affair in this prefecture.

Prefecture of Lassithi
Here we have the Liatiko grape variety cultivated in the vineyards of 34 communities. 70% of this variety is cultivated at an altitude of 350 meters. The prefecture yields the Siteia appellation of origin wine.

• Siteia Area
This area comprises the vineyards of 18 villages, the most important of which are those of the town of Siteia and Piskocephalo. The area is selected for the Siteia Red wine, which is made from the Liatiko grape variety. The types of wine produced are: Red dry, Red naturally sweet, Red sweet. The sugar content for the dry type is not more than 188gr/lt, 221gr/lt for the sweet and 238gr/lt for the naturally sweet. The yield should not be in excess of 800gr of grapes per 1,000m2 of vineyard.

Prefecture of Rethymnon
The dominant grape varieties are: Liatiko, Tsardana and Vidiano. Production of wine is small in this prefecture and grape wines are fermented by the farmers at home.

WINERIES AND VINEYARDS OF CRETE

EAS OF KISSAMOS
Winery of Kasteli, Kissamos
Tel.: 28220 22508

CENTRAL UNION OF HANIA
Winery of Kolymbari, Crete
Tel.: 28240 22448

MICHALAKIS BROS S.A.
Industrial Area of Heraklion, Sector D'
71408 Heraklion, Crete (visitors allowed)
Tel.: 2810 381303, fax: 2810 381183
Branch in Athens: 87 Makrygianni Street, 18233
Ayios Ioannis, Renti
Tel.: 210 4929800,fax: 210 381183

M. MILIARAKIS – M. MARAGAKIS LTD – OINOTROPOS
Industrial Area of Heraklion, Sector S'
Tel.: 2810 381359

VENOVIN-ALEXAKIS & SONS S.A.
Eirinis & Filias 104, 71500 Peridi Metochi,
Heraklion, Crete
Tel. : 2810 252019

VINS DE CRETE I. PAPAGEORGIOU, I. HARKOUTSIS
70011 Venerato, Heraklion, Crete
Tel. 2810 791801, fax 2810 792108

AGROTIKOS SYNETERISMOS ARCHANON
Winery of Ano Archanes, Heraklion, Crete
Tel.: 2810 751834

ENOSI PEZON – EAS PEZON
P.O. BOX 1077, 70100 Kalloni, Heraklion, Crete
(visitors allowed)
Tel.: 2810 741202-204, fax 2810 741528
www.pezaunion.gr

MINOS WINES OF CRETE S.A. - MICHALAKI BROS
70100 Peza of Heraklion, Crete
Tel.: 2810 741213, 741595-6, fax 2810 741597
(visitors allowed)

G. PATERIANAKIS S.A. – MELISSOKEPOS S.A.
Winery at Melesses, Municipality of Nikos Kazantzakis
P.O. Box 1125 71001, Melesses (visitors allowed)
Offices: 7 Zographou Street, 71201 Heraklion, Crete
Tel.: 2810 284689, fax 2810 226673

CRETA OLYMPIAS S.A.
Winery at Kounavoi, 70100 Heraklion, Crete
(visitors allowed)
Tel.: 2810 741431, fax 2810 741323
e-mail: Creta-olympias@her.forthnet.gr
Offices: 330 Theseos Street, 17675 Kalithea
Tel: 210 9419279, fax 210 9403282

GEA S.A. – KTIMA LYRARAKI
Winery at Alagni, Monofatsi, Heraklion, Crete
(visitors allowed)
Offices: 92, G. Papandreou Street, Heraklion
Tel: 2810 284614, fax 2810 288515

SYNETERISMOS HERAKLIOU
Winery at Dafnes, Heraklion, Crete
Tel.: 2810 250164

EAS SITEIAS – SITEIA WINES
Winery on the 3rd km from Siteia to Heraklion,
Siteia 72300
(visitors allowed)
Tel.: 28430 25200,29350,fax 28430 3156
Offices: 74 Mysonos Street, Siteia
Tel. 28430 22211, 23331, 22954. fax 23222

IOANNIS H. OIKONOMOU
Winery at Zeros, Siteia 72039
(visitors allowed)
Tel.: 28430 91235
Offices: 102 Emm. Stavrakaki, 72300 Siteia

BOUTARI KTIMA – FANTAXOMETOHO
70100 Skalani, Heraklion
(visitors allowed)
Tel.: 2810 731617

NOSTOS – MANOUSAKI WINERY
Organic Viticulture
At Vatolakos, Hania
Tel.: 28210 60216, fax 28210 28123
e-mail: kgalan@otenet.gr

IOANNIS DIGENAKIS
7, Kantakouzinon Str & Michael Psellou, 71307
Heraklion
Tel.: 2810 233999, 322846, 233623
fax 2810 211466
e-mail: digenakis@her.forthnet.gr
Web site: www.digenakis.gr

Drinks and sweets from Must – Wine – Raki

RAKI LIQUOR
(with honey, cinnamon and orange rind)

INGREDIENTS

1 lt raki

3 tablespoons honey

2 cinnamon sticks

1 teaspoon cloves

2 large pieces of orange rind

DIRECTIONS

1. Buy a large bottle, run water to clean it inside and let it drain. In this bottle you will put the cinnamon, cloves and orange rinds and top them with raki.

2. Seal the bottle and keep it at a cool place in the house for at least 2 months. In the meanwhile, shake the bottle to dissolve the honey.

RAKI
(with savory, thyme, cinnamon and cloves)

INGREDIENTS

4 lt raki

2 1/2 cups sugar

1 tablespoon cloves

4 large cinnamon sticks

2 cups thyme (leaves and sprigs)

2 cups savory (leaves and sprigs)

DIRECTIONS

1. Use a large glass jar of 4 lt capacity. Place the cinnamon, cloves, thyme, savory, sugar and add the raki.

2. Seal the jar air-tight and let it stand in the sun for 40 days.

3. Serve this drink iced or warm (infused with sage)

MOUSTALEVRIA
WITH FLOUR or NISESTE
(10 small bowls)

INGREDIENTS

8 glasses must, not boiled

2-3 tablespoons sugar (in a pouch)

1 1/2 kg flour or 2 glasses niseste

walnuts, coarsely ground

sesame, roasted

cinnamon, grated

DIRECTIONS

1. We get the must from white grapes and boil it in a large pot for 5 minutes. Stir to avoid clotting. Add the sugar pouch (tied to handle) and lower heat. A thick foam accumulates on the surface of the must. Skim the foam using a perforated spoon, until the must remains a transparent liquid.

2. Remove the pot from heat and let the must rest for 3-4 hours, and then pass it through a fine colander or strainer or cloth. Place the must in a clean non-stick pot. If you put the pot back on the heat, it will gradually turn darker.

3. To make moustalevria we allow the must to boil only for ten minutes, then lower the heat and add flour or niseste (1 glass flour/niseste for 4 glasses must). We dissolve the flour in a little cold must and slowly add this mixture to the pot, stirring at the same time using a wooden ladle.

4. When the must starts coagulating, forming bubbles on top, we remove it using a ladle and place it in little bowls sprinkled with grated walnuts and sesame. When the must in the bowls is at room temperature, we top it with a little cinnamon and grated walnuts.

BARLEY ROLLS / COOKIES
30-40 rolls

INGREDIENTS

2 cups olive oil

1 1/2 cups sugar

1 cup orange juice

1/2 cup raki

1 cup brandy

1 tablespoon soda

1 tablespoon baking powder

1 teaspoon cinnamon

3-4 cloves, grated

1 kg white flour

1 1/2 kg barley flour

DIRECTIONS

1. Use a large bowl to pour in the olive oil and sugar. Mix them for 5 minutes using your hands to dissolve the sugar in the olive oil. Then add the orange juice, raki, soda (dissolved in the brandy), cinnamon, cloves and mix them with your hands for 5 minutes.

2. Add to the above mixture the baking powder, white and barley flour (alternating between the two in one cup instalments). Knead well to mix all ingredients and get medium hardness dough that does not stick to the sides of the bowl and to your hands.

3. Pick approximately 1/2 handful of dough and roll it to a cylinder, 7-9cm long and 1 1/2 cm thick. Find the middle and bend the cylinder to form a circle. Repeat until you have exhausted the dough or reached the required number of rolls. Place them on a baking sheet lined with greaseproof paper and bake them in a preheated oven at 180°C for 45 minutes approximately.

THE BEST TRADITIONAL PRODUCTS AND WHERE TO FIND THEM

"KRITIKI YI"

Meaning Cretan Land. This is a small industry producing traditional pasta from fresh milk and local grown wheat. The owner is Mrs. Marentaki-Psomataki, Philia and the business is located at Ayios Georgios, Grambousa of Kissamos, prefecture of Hania, Crete.
Tel. 28220-24091.

"O FOURNOS TIS SEVASTIS"

(Sevasti's Bakery):
This business is located in the village of Episkopi 15 km south of the town of Heraklion. There you can find traditional bakery products, the famous koulouropoulia, small rusk bites made from patent barley and cumin.
Tel. 2810-771477.

"TO XOBLIASTO KOULOURAKI" (The Ornate Bagel):

This business produces the best traditional loaves of ornate bread

offered to guests during wedding, christening and other ceremonies. Please note that preparation of these loaves takes a week to complete. The business is located at the village of Marathos, in the province of Malevyzi.
Tel. 2810-521051.

"KORFIANA KALOLOIDIA" (Goodies from Koryfes):

This cottage business produces very tasty and crunchy biscuits. The 'krasata' type biscuits/rolls are made from olive oil and red wine. The delicious barley rolls are baked in a wood-fired oven and taste delicious. The business is located at the village of Koryfes, province of Malevyzi.
Tel. 2810-851282.

"ASSITIANA EDESMATA" (Delicacies from Assites):

Home-made bread, barley rolls, kalitsounia, preserve, biscuits from organic grown wheat/barley, sauce, pickles, *xerotigana* (fritters). The business is located at the village of Kato Assites, municipality of Gorgolaini.
Tel. 2810-801568.

"MELISANTHI":

This is the name for a women's agrarian association specializing in traditional pastries: *kalistounia, lychnarakia, sousamades,* stuffed biscuits, rusks for dipping and sarikopites (pies). The business is located at the village of Ayios Myron, municipality of Gorgolaini.
Tel. 2810-722038.

"PARADOSI" (Tradition):

Barley rurks, traditional buns/bread and kalitsounia. The business is located at the village of Preveliana, municipality of Ayia Varvara.
Tel. 28940-22637.

"TO MYROVOLON":

This shop sells local wine and tsikoudia, grape juice syrup, local cheese, hand-made pasta, preserve and marmalade, Cretan rusks, home-made soap bars, a.o. The majority of these products are produced

and standardized by the same business with the distinctive name VAMOS Plc. The business is located at the village of Vamos.
Tel. 28250-23100 / 23250.

"KRITIKI YI Co." (Cretan Land):

This is the trade name of a business run by two sisters and registered by the name Mavromatidi-Polychronaki Eugenia. The business produces and markets excellent vinegar made from local wine, an assortment of rusks (some stuffed with almonds), seven-leavened bread, herbs, etc.
Tel: 6972262469.

WOMEN'S AGRARIAN ASSOCIATION OF GAVALOHORI

This picturesque village in the province of Hania is known for its handicraft products (lace making using bobbinets). You will find a wide variety of laced cloth, including table cloths, but also home-made marmalade. This business is located at Gavalohori, right at the center of the village.
Tel: 28250-22038.

"TO XATHERI":

In the Cretan dialect xatheri means 'exceptional' or 'excellent'. The story behind this cottage business is this: Mrs. Maria Pitsikaki from the village of Ayia Irini, in the municipality of Kroussonas, compiled all the recipes her grandmother had entrusted her through the years and, putting extra love and care, plus prime quality ingredients, she managed to produce delicious products: biscuits (stuffed with almonds, currants and orange rind), barley rusks/rolls for diabetics, cookies made from sesame and aniseed, hard bread, olive paste and other dainty morsels with mastic.
Tel.: 2810-762991/ 2810 211-794.

AGROTOURISM ACCOMMODATION UNITS WITH A TASTE

PREFECTURE OF HANIA

Vamos S.A.

This accommodation unit comprises twenty houses that have been restored to accommodate from 2 to 7 guests. Each house features its own garden and stone-paved patio. In summer this accommodation unit organizes various cultural and agrotourism activities and guests are invited to participate. It is located at the village of Vamos, area of Apokoronou.
Tel. 28250-23250,
www.vamossa.gr/.

Kamares

Although built in the place of a Venetian glebe; it still bears the architectural characteristics of the era that followed the period of Venetian rule – Turkish occupation. This accommodation is located in the village of Mahairoi with a view to two imposing ravines. In the hotel's garden, under banana trees, hortensias and jasmines the guests enjoy a nourishing breakfast made from local, organic grown products.
Address: Hotel Kamares, Mahairoi Apokoronou, Crete.
Tel: 28250-41111,
www.otenet.gr/kamares/

Elia

A 200-year old house has been converted into a magnificent guesthouse retaining the stone masonry, stone arches and wooden staircases. Its large garden hosts scores of olive trees and fruit trees. Its cuisine remains faithful to the Cretan diet. Address: ANO VOUVES, KOLYMVARI 73006, HANIA-CRETE, GREECE.
Tel. 28240-83056,
Web: www.elia-crete.com.gr.

Milia

This accommodation comprises thirteen stone-built houses in the center of a private grove of chestnut and arbutus trees at an altitude of 500m. One of the houses functions as a restaurant with a fireplace and long benches. All food is made from organic products grown in the garden.
Address: Milia (5 km from Vlatos), Hania, Crete, Greece.
Tel. 28220-51569, 28210-46774.
Web:www.in.gr/agro/vacation/milia.

PREFECTURE OF RETHYMNON

ENAGRON FARM

A few years ago Mr. Yannis Papadakis and his wife Fani decided to return to their birth place, the village of Axos. In an area of 30K m2 they built their home which they latter extended with housing units and facilities to turn the entire complex into a tourist accommodation unit. The Enagron Farm started its operations in 2001. In its gardens the owners grow organic vegetables free from pesticides. The currants and wine are produced from their own vineyards. In the farm roam domesticated animals: chicken, geese, ducks, horses, sheep and goats. The owners place a great emphasis on the Cretan cuisine. Guests will have to opportunity to taste the apaki, stuffed cabbage leaves, Cretan sausages, rabbit stew with nuts and salad made from wild greens. Address: village of Axos, Rethymnon, Crete.
Tel: 28430-61611,61618.
E-mail:. info@cretanatural.com.
Web: www.enagron.gr.

Rodialos Mansion

Rodialos is a mansion located in the Northern coast of Crete near the village of Panormon, right in the middle of the island, upon one of the so many rocky shores of Crete. The mansion is built in the middle of a wide private field. Its architecture, painting techniques and colors follow the style of the Minoan palaces discovered on Crete. If you are interested in learning more about the Cretan diet, the owner of Rodialos, Mrs. Mary Fragiadaki organizes courses in Cretan cuisine. Address: Rodialos Mansion, Panormo, Xirokambos area, Rethymnon, Crete, Greece.
Tel.: 28340-51310.
Web: www.rodialos.gr

LEFKOREITIS

Right at the center of the Askyfou plateau Mr. Nikos Kalogerakis has built an accommodation complex consisting of 13 rooms with a view to the plateau. The cuisine of this unit offers traditional meals: delicious tsigariasto (sauté meat), Sfakian pies, staka with eggs, apaki, partridge in red sauce or with staka, pheasant and quail meat. On the plateau you will have the opportunity to ride a unique local breed of horses known as 'georgalidika'.
Tel. 28250-95455.

PREFECTURE OF HERAKLION
Agioklima

This guesthouse is a restored building of the 19th century, property of the Troulinos family. It is located on a hill top at the village of Petrokephalo, 15 km from the town of Heraklion, at an altitude of 340m. Guests have the opportunity to cook their own meals in the wood-fired oven and taste the home-made raki with a view to Mt. Psiloreitis. Address: Agioklima Guesthouse, Petrokephalo, Heraklion, Crete, Greece.
Tel.: 2810-223861. Web: www.agioklima.gr

The Viglatoras Traditional House

The Viglatoras is a traditional farm house set in a lush, little village Sarhos, at the foot of Mt. Pseiloritis, 20 km from the town of Heraklion. The farm covers an area of 7.3 acres and offers a Cretan cuisine. Address: Viglatoras, Sarchos, Heraklion, Crete, Greece.
Tel.: 2810-711332, 252581, 811654. Web: www.viglatoras.gr